MAN and ANIMALS

Living, Working and Changing Together

In Celebration of the 100th Anniversary

THE SCHOOL OF VETERINARY MEDICINE

University of Pennsylvania

Contributions by

David Anthony
Arjun Appadurai
Pam Crabtree
Maude de Schauensee
Peter Dodson
Pamela Hearne
John Martin
Richard Meadow
David O'Connor
Donald Patterson
Gregory Possehl
Jennifer Quick
Mary Voigt

Published by
THE UNIVERSITY MUSEUM
University of Pennsylvania
1984

This catalogue is presented in part
through the generosity of **Kal Kan**

**Library of Congress Cataloging in
Publication Data**
Main entry under title:
Man and animals.
  Bibliography: p. 80
  1. Domestic animals—History—
Exhibitions. 2. University of Pennsylva-
nia. School of Veterinary Medicine—
History—Exhibitions. 3. University of
Pennsylvania. University Museum—
Exhibitions. I. Anthony, David. II. Uni-
versity of Pennsylvania. University
Museum.
SF114.U6P486 1984
636'.0074'014811 84–19501
ISBN 0-934718-68-7

MAN and ANIMALS

Living, Working and Changing Together

CONTENTS

This catalogue has been produced in conjunction with the exhibition *Man and Animals: Living, Working and Changing Together*, held at **The University Museum** from October 4, 1984, through June 30, 1985.

ACKNOWLEDGMENTS

The University Museum is moving toward its Centennial, to be celebrated in 1986-87. In the course of formulating our plans for this festive year, it became increasingly clear that the decade of the 1880s was one of extraordinary vitality and change at the University of Pennsylvania. One of the most significant of these changes was the founding of our renowned School of Veterinary Medicine. This is now one of the University's internationally recognized centers of excellence. It is thus a pleasure for me to have this opportunity to join with Dean Robert Marshak in organizing the exhibition *Man and Animals: Living, Working and Changing Together.*

This exhibition has proved to be an extremely interesting venture for our two institutions. We have found a common ground in the history of domesticated animals and the nature of biological change. Our approaches, however, are quite different, and this has given a special opportunity for learning to those who have been deeply involved in the creation of the exhibition. I especially want to make note of the cooperation our Exhibits and Publications staffs have had from Dr. Donald Patterson, Dr. John Martin and Dr. Peter Dodson of the Veterinary School. Much of the inspiration for the exhibition and this catalogue has come from their insights into the human-animal relationship. In addition, Mrs. Bonnie Dalzell of the School of Veterinary Medicine provided special assistance in arranging for the loan of the dog skeletons. Dr. Jeffrey Wortman, also of the School, was responsible for taking and reading the radiographs of the cat mummies. The chromosome preparations of the dog and cat were made by Steven Wilson of the Section of Medical Genetics.

It is also fitting for me to recognize the contribution that the scientific staff of The University Museum has made to this endeavor. I want to especially thank Dr. David O'Connor for his research on the cat in ancient Egypt, Mrs. Pamela Hearne for supplying material on the native dogs of America, Miss Maude de Schauensee for her material on the horse and the dog in the ancient Near East and Drs. Gregory Possehl and Arjun Appadurai for the section on the cow in Indian culture. Dr. Mary Voigt also contributed material on the Near East, providing information and guidance on the dog burial from her site of Hajji Firuz. Mr. David Anthony's expertise on the domestication of the horse is also reflected in this catalogue. Mr. Richard Meadow of Harvard University made a fine contribution to this publication as well as playing an invaluable role in securing the loan of the Jaguar Cave dog specimens from the Museum of Comparative Zoology at Harvard. Dr. Pam Crabtree has been kind enough to review a great deal of material as the project evolved.

The Museum's Conservation Laboratory, under the supervision of Virginia Greene, and the Photographic Studio, with Harmer Fred Schoch as Chief Photographer, made their usual splendid contributions to the success of the exhibit and the presentation of the materials that accompany these undertakings. The Publications Division of the Museum produced this fine exhibition catalogue. Jennifer Quick has taken the draft copy for the exhibition labels and the text for this publication and produced the admirably understandable prose that follows this preface; Martha Phillips has done the beautiful layout; and Barbara Murray has guided the project through all stages of preparation.

Finally, the Exhibits Department under the direction of John T. Murray, ably assisted by Stephen Oliver and George Bucher, has given us one more spectacular show. Additional help was given by Janet Monge who prepared casts and tended to some of the more fragile skeletal remains.

This list of thanks and recognition could go on and on. There were objects loaned, transportation arranged and a host of other activities that have come together through the efforts of the Registrar's Office under Irene Romano to make this exhibition a success. We thank you all, everyone who worked together to ensure the splendid results.

Robert H. Dyson, Jr.
Director
The University Museum

George Bucher (l.) and Jack Murray of the Exhibits Department with the scale model for the exhibition *Man and Animals: Living, Working and Changing Together.*

Stephen Oliver of the Exhibits Department working on the display of a dog skeleton.

INTRODUCTION

Archaeologists and anthropologists frequently speak of three great revolutions in human history: the evolution of the genus *Homo*, the development of farming and stock breeding or the food-producing revolution, and the advent of cities. The search for the earliest farming communities, and the remains of their domesticated plants and animals, has been one of the most provocative problems on which archaeologists have worked during the years following World War II. Important advances in our knowledge of both the history and cultural processes involved in this story of human achievement have been made in the Near East, Southeast Asia, Mesoamerica and the western coast of South America.

Detail of a drawing of a 9th century B.C. Assyrian relief showing horses in their stable drinking and being groomed.

(From *The Monuments of Nineveh, from Drawings Made on the Spot* by A. H. Layard, Vol. 1, Pl. 30. London:1849.)

Many of the most useful animals seem to have been domesticated in the Near East, as well as in regions bordering on this immense geographic area, from 10,000 to 12,000 years ago. We have selected four of these as the focus for this exhibition: the horse, dog, cow and cat. They represent animals with a wide spectrum of importance, from pets to major food producers and powerful draft animals that have provided energy for human endeavors over many millennia.

A domesticated animal is different from its wild counterpart. These differences are a part of its genetic makeup and are not traits that have been acquired over a single animal's lifetime. These genetic changes came into being through selective breeding by man for animals that suited his purposes, be it the availability of meat, the need for traction or the desire for companionship. Over the course of several, possibly many, animal generations, man preserved and allowed to reproduce those animals which filled these needs, while the reproduction of others of the species was curtailed. Thus, the genetic makeup of entire populations of animals was shifted from a wild composition to a new one. Lacking an understanding of genetics, early human societies brought about these changes not by a deliberate plan, but by the chance combination of genetic variation existing in the available stock, and perhaps to some extent by the intuitive recognition that 'like begets like.' Domesticated animals are thus a human creation and can be thought of as living artifacts.

The common domestic animals today are quite different from their wild progenitors. Each domesticated species as we now know it consists of a number of breeds, each distinguished by its own physical and behavioral characteristics. Some of the changes associated with domestication were apparent early. A number of different types of cattle and dogs can be seen in Egyptian paintings from as early as 2000 B.C. The most dramatic changes associated with domestication, however, have been produced in the past 100 to 200 years by selectively breeding for special purposes, utilizing in many cases knowledge of genetics and modern theories of animal breeding. As a result, we now have a large variety of dairy and beef cattle; draft, pleasure and race horses; and a myriad of dog breeds differing remarkably in size, shape and behavioral repertoires. Cats have undergone less dramatic change, but a number of new breeds have been introduced.

Through domestication, man has significantly molded wild species of animals for his own purposes. In the process, human societies have been changed as well. The evolution of human enterprise has been closely tied to the practical value of domesticated animals for food, clothing, power and transportation. Beyond the utilitarian matters, it is apparent in art and literature and in the place of pets in many cultures today, that the companionship of animals fills an important human psychological need.

HORSE

Half-bred mare

Ceramic rhyton
Ardebil area, Iran
150 B.C. – A.D. 250
63-15-1
H. 19.3 cm.   L. 27.2 cm

This rhyton or drinking vessel is thought to come from the Ardebil area of northwestern Iran. It is in the form of a stylized horse equipped with trappings. These include a bridle with a strap down the center of the face and a saddle cloth held in place with straps around the chest and under the tail. These straps are decorated with pendants. Saddlecloths were used for riding as saddles were unknown at this time in the Near East.

The Fossil Record

Horses have a long and distinguished lineage. Fossil remains from five continents (excluding only Australia and Antarctica) have been linked together in an evolutionary scheme that traces the horse's descent from 60 million years ago to the present. Current studies of the fossil record involve sites in the eastern Mediterranean, the Near East and east Africa.

Although the earliest fossils were first found in Europe, subsequent discoveries in North America established it as the center of horse evolution. Horses flourished in great abundance and diversity on what are now the Great Plains, and survived there until about eight thousand years ago when they became extinct. Remains of the earliest horse, *Hyracotherium* or *Eohippus* (the dawn horse), have been found in Europe and in western North America, especially in Wyoming. The dawn horse was small, standing only 10 inches to 20 inches at the shoulders (withers), with a short face and simple low-crowned teeth adapted for browsing on soft-leafed forest vegetation. It had four toes and one vestige (splint) on its front feet, and three toes and two splints on its hind feet.

Forty million years later, as primeval forests began to give way to great grasslands, a new lineage of horses evolved in North America. They were considerably larger than the dawn horse, and their teeth were equipped with a series of complex ridges that made them well suited for feeding on tough, abrasive grasses. These horses had three toes, with the central toe the most prominent, and their lower limbs had become longer and specialized for speed. They began to run and trot like modern horses. By the time they were living entirely on open grasslands where the ground is firm, they had developed the ability to run on tip-toe.

After another 10 million years, *Hipparion*, perhaps the most successful of the three-toed grazing horses, arose in North America. This horse migrated across the great land bridge (Beringia) from Alaska to Siberia, and spread across Eurasia into Africa where it lasted until the Pleistocene, less than 2 million years ago. In North America, ancestors of the true horse continued to live and evolve. The three-toed horse was succeeded by *Pliohippus*, the first horse with a single enlarged toe on each foot. Then, during the Pleistocene, single-toed horses belonging to the modern genus *Equus* evolved from *Pliohippus*.

During the Ice Age at the end of the Pleistocene, large herds of horses (*Equus ferus*) roamed the open plains of Europe, Asia and North America. By approximately eight thousand years ago, the great ice sheets had melted, the forests were re-established, and horses for reasons still unknown had disappeared from North America and northern and western Europe. They persisted in central Asia and survive to the present in Mongolia. Przewalski's horse, the sole surviving descendant of the Pleistocene horse, was first discovered in Mongolia in 1879. It is regarded as the wild progenitor of the domestic horse.

Living Equids

The family *Equidae* today comprises the single-toed horse. All living equids are included in the genus *Equus* and are members of the subfamily *Equinae*. There are six living species of wild equids: three African zebras (Grevy's, Burchell's and Mountain); the African

Artist's rendering of *Eohippus*.

The Bering Land Bridge (Beringia) as reconstructed by the latest research. Ancestors of both the dog and the horse traveled across this bridge.

(After Jason Smith)

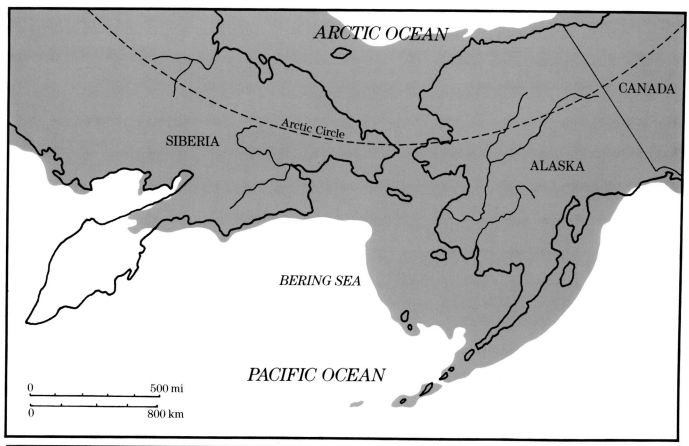

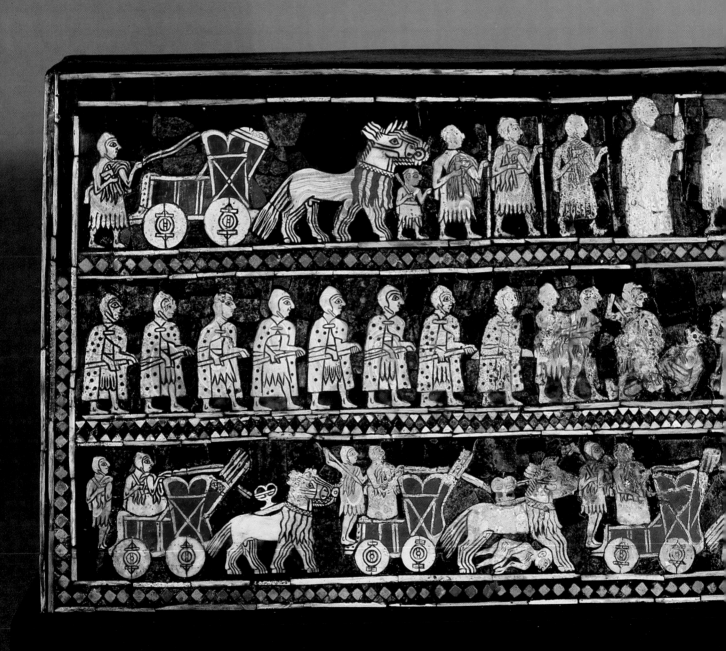

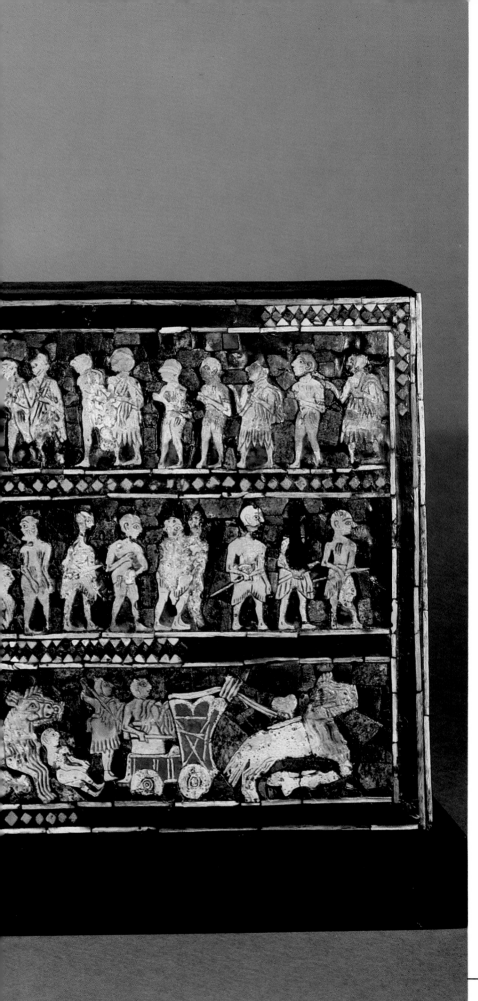

'Standard'
Shell, lapis lazuli, red sandstone
and bitumen
Ur, Iraq
Ca. 2600–2500 B.C.
Courtesy of The Trustees of The
British Museum, London

The 'Standard' was found in a grave
in the so-called Royal Cemetery at
Ur. One side depicts peaceful scenes
and subjects, while the side shown
in this photograph apparently
represents war. It is also one of the
earliest representations of equids in
use as draft animals in the Near
East.

In the bottom register, groups of
four equids are shown pulling carts
which have four wooden wheels,
each made of three solid planks
joined together. The equids are controlled by rings in their noses and
wear collars, set high on their
necks, that take the weight of the
pulling. Neither procedure works
well on equids as the high position
of the collar curtails the animals'
ability to breathe while pulling, and
equid noses are not suited for rings.

wild ass; the Asiatic half-ass (known variously as onager, kulan or kiang); and the Mongolian wild horse or Przewalski's horse mentioned above. The two domesticated species derived from wild equids are the donkey (*Equus asinus asinus*) and the horse (*Equus caballus*).

Wild equids are generally small, typically 50 inches or less at the withers, with relatively large angular heads, short robust limbs and long tails that have long hairs only at their ends. The mane is usually stiff and erect, and there is no forelock. Ears are notably longer than in domestic horses. Necks are thick and short, and head carriage is lower than in horses. Withers are comparatively weak, and the rump (croup) may be higher than the withers. Hoofs generally are small, compact and very tough.

Equids differ markedly from one another in their chromosome counts, but hybrids can be produced. Thus crosses can be made between horse and ass (producing mules and hinnies), horse and onager, horse and zebra, and ass and zebra. In almost all cases, however, the offspring are sterile. Such interbreeding probably almost never occurs in nature.

Early History of the Horse

There is general agreement among students of the subject that horses were first domesticated about 4000 B.C. in the coastal plain region above the Black Sea, in what is now the Ukrainian republic of the USSR. The horses involved looked very much like Przewalski's horse. Such horses were accurately portrayed by Palaeolithic cave painters and, in about 3000 B.C., were elegantly pictured on vessels such as a silver vase from the Maikop culture in the region just north of the Caucasus mountains in Russia.

Horses were the last of the major animals to be domesticated and have undergone the least genetic modification. There is essentially no skeletal evidence indicative of the domestication process, for there was no decrease in body size such as that which accompanied domestication of cattle from the giant aurochs. The earliest episode of horse domestication was brought about for dietary purposes: horses were kept for slaughter, like cattle and pigs. Subsequently, horses were employed for draft, using the technology already applied to cattle, and later still they were ridden. Thus, both dietary and technological factors were probably involved in the domestication process. Horse-head effigies and the remains of horse-related rituals in the graves and settlements of the people in southern Russia who first tamed horses suggest that man developed a special appreciation or even reverence toward these animals at a very early date.

Wild horses might have seemed unlikely candidates for domestication. They were skittish, alert and suspicious. Stallions kept closely guarded harems of up to 15 or 20 mares, over whom they fought in vicious (and occasionally mortal) combat. At the same time, wild horses possessed other traits that predisposed them to become highly satisfactory domesticates. Bands were held together by extremely strong bonds of dominance-obedience, loyalty and mutual affection, much like the bonding mechanisms exhibited in wolf packs. As with wolves, all that was required was to redirect the animal's natural bonding instincts toward humans, and the result was a very loyal, affectionate domesticate. The same social bonds do not seem to have characterized wild cattle, sheep or pigs, and none

Zebra

Ass

Onager

Przewalski's Horse

Domestic Horse

of these animals has attached itself to humans in quite the same manner as horses and dogs. These bonding traits suggest that domestication of the horse might have proceeded surprisingly quickly once the process was begun.

Early Domesticators of the Horse

The human societies responsible for the first domestication of the horse were the Dnieper-Donets culture, which first arose between ca. 5000–4500 B.C., and the Sredni Stog culture, which appeared ca. 4000 B.C. These were the distant ancestors of the nomadic Cimmerians and Scythians of Eurasia.

The Dnieper-Donets culture was distributed over a large territory in southern Russia, north of the Black Sea. The natural environment in this area was highly diverse, encompassing mountains, densely forested plateaus and an arid coastal plain or steppe. In the transitional forest-steppe zone, even slight changes in precipitation, runoff, temperature or even human population densities could trigger drastic ecological changes that in turn might require significant cultural adaptations. The Dnieper-Donets culture appears to have gradually emerged in this ecologically sensitive zone. These people adopted horticulture and stockbreeding, mainly of cattle but also of sheep and pig, in an effort to intensify food production to support a rising population. As populations continued to expand, more and more areas of forest were cleared, resulting in the decline

Plaster cast of limestone plaque
Khafaje, Iraq
Ca. 2600–2500 B.C.
Lent by The Oriental Institute, Chicago

The lower register of this votive plaque shows part of a scene of equids pulling a vehicle. The pole of the vehicle, with the rein guide in place on it, is like that shown on two objects from Ur—the limestone relief and the 'Standard.' This pole, as well as the type and position of the fringed collars around the animals' necks, indicates that a vehicle is being drawn, although this section of the scene is now lost. The heads of the animals (missing from the Ur plaque) resemble very closely those of the animals on the 'Standard' which have been identified as equids. These representations thus provide evidence that equids were used as draft animals in at least two cities in Mesopotamia at this early date. (The original of the plaque is in Baghdad.)

Man and Animals

Limestone plaque
Ur, Iraq
Ca. 2600–2500 B.C.
CBS 17086
H. 13.0 cm.   W. 26.8 cm.

This votive limestone plaque carved in low relief is one of earliest representations of equids used as draft animals. Here, apparently four equids are shown under one yoke, pulling a cart with two solid wheels. The driver walks behind the vehicle. As was usual at this time, the equids were hitched with collars placed high on their necks, revealing the adaptation of the yoke from use on bovids to which to was well suited. Owing to differences in anat-omy, this was a crude and ineffi-cient procedure for harnessing equids, for the pulling strap was placed so that it cut off their breathing. In more recent times, this has been corrected through the use of the horse collar which lowers the point of stress to the chest of the animal. A plaque from Khafaje, Iraq, with a very similar scene, shows the heads of the equids which are broken away on this plaque.

Chart showing the evolution of the horse's skull, legs and feet, from *Eohippus* through the modern genus *Equus*. Dates given are for beginnings of epochs in years Before Present.

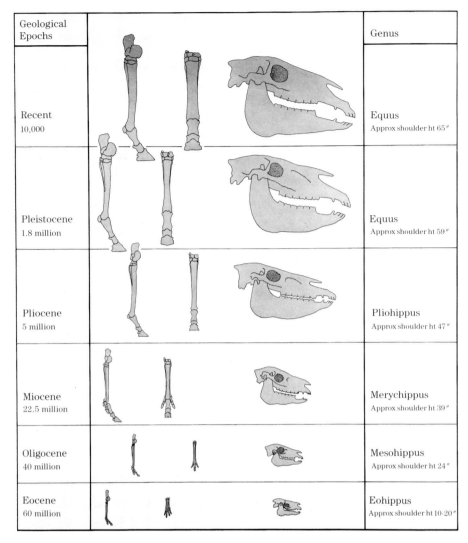

Geological Epochs		Genus
Recent 10,000		Equus Approx shoulder ht 65″
Pleistocene 1.8 million		Equus Approx shoulder ht 59″
Pliocene 5 million		Pliohippus Approx shoulder ht 47″
Miocene 22.5 million		Merychippus Approx shoulder ht 39″
Oligocene 40 million		Mesohippus Approx shoulder ht 24″
Eocene 60 million		Eohippus Approx shoulder ht 10-20″

of forest game animals. By 4500–4000 B.C., increasing competition for the dwindling resources of river valleys and steppe borderland forests pushed some weaker groups of people into the outer edges of the arid grasslands. These communities were forced to exploit steppe food resources, the most abundant of which was the wild horse population. Wild horse bands were probably driven into hidden enclosures or corrals during communal hunts. A successful drive might net more horses than could immediately be consumed and the extras might be kept alive in the corrals. Since it is easier to utilize captive animals than to expend energy in hunting, a transition to horse herding would have been a logical step for people already adept at cattle herding. Thus the Dnieper-Donets culture opened up a new environmental zone to efficient human exploitation and soon produced the world's first domesticated horse.

Around 4000 B.C., a climatic shift brought markedly colder conditions to Europe. Horses, however, are supremely adapted to survive cold weather. Their tough hoofs allow them to break through the ice on frozen water holes, their high gait allows them to move through snows that immobilize cattle and sheep, and they feed by using their hoofs to paw the snow away from the grass beneath.

Cattle and sheep use their noses to push snow away, and in deep snow their noses will become so raw and bloody that they will starve unless provided with fodder. So horses, first domesticated by marginal hunting groups, now became accepted as reliable, cold-adapted stock by a much wider range of communities.

These developments led to the emergence at about this same time (the 4th millennium B.C.) of a horse-breeding culture that was more mobile, more concerned with settlement defense and more deeply involved in foreign trade: the Sredni Stog culture. Faunal remains from excavated sites indicate that horses supplied almost half the meat diet of these people. Analysis of the horse bones has resulted in their identification as domesticated specimens. In addition, curved antler tines pierced by holes have been found and are interpreted as cheekpieces for bits; one was found in connection with a ritual horse head-and-hide deposit. Other artifactual remains indicate contact with neighboring cultures. These contacts might well have been related to a burgeoning trade in domesticated horses, for it was about this time that horses began to appear in significant numbers in eastern and central Europe and in the Caucasus, the region between the Black and Caspian Seas. From the Caucasus, horses were eventually traded into the Near East, arriving during the late Akkadian period (ca. 2200 B.C.).

Horses in the Near East

Archaeological and skeletal evidence documents the spread of equids in the Near East, but such evidence must be interpreted cautiously, for not only are three species present (horse, ass and onager), but hybrids among all of them complicate the picture. All of these equids which were not true horses make difficult the task of isolating the history of the domestic horse; however, a general outline can be drawn from available information.

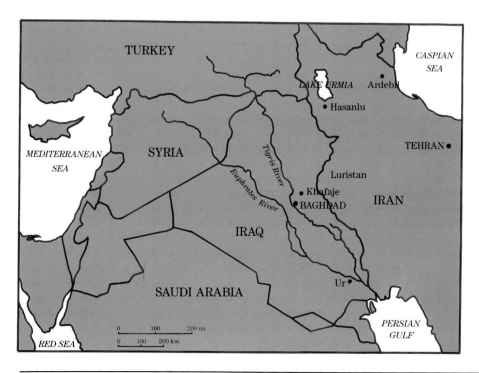

Map of the Near East indicating archaeological sites which have provided information on the early history of the horse.

The earliest evidence for what appear to be wheeled vehicles, rather crude roofed sledges, comes from Uruk in southern Mesopotamia, dated to ca. 3200 B.C. These vehicles, however, were drawn by cattle. Representations and texts from various sites confirm the existence of domestic herds of equids and discuss breeding, feeding and plowing, but there is little firm evidence that the principal equids were horses. On the contrary, horses were apparently still very rare. Equids used in draft were hitched like cattle; however, due to the anatomical dissimilarity of equids and cattle, this was an inefficient and crude procedure. Slightly later there appear pictorial representations of men riding bareback on what may be equids which are controlled with nose rings. Around 2600–2500 B.C., equids used for draft are shown with nose rings in scenes on the 'Standard' of Ur (a site in Iraq). Later in the 2nd millennium, paired reins were developed. These were attached to a bit made of soft material. Reins afforded a far greater control of braking and of a horse's directional movement.

Around 2000–1600 B.C., horses became widespread from Anatolia to Egypt and Nubia, and the single-axled, spoke-wheeled chariot appeared, particularly in Babylonia. A team of two horses, harnessed by a yoke, was used to pull the chariot. Chariots were probably not used in battle, however, for there was room for only one passenger and the demands of controlling the team, maneuvering the vehicle, and fighting were incompatible.

At this time, there is also ample documentation of riding, not only of horses, but particularly of other equids. The bareback riders were always male, and were often lightly clothed or naked. They

(opposite)
Copper or bronze horse trappings
Hasanlu, Iran
Ca. 1000–800 B.C.
73-5-315, 73-5-545, 73-5-547,
73-5-548, 73-5-552a,b, – 73-5-555

Horse trappings of several types and materials were found at Hasanlu. They were buried in buildings destroyed when the town was sacked and burned by invaders at the end of the 9th century B.C. None were found in position on the horse skeletons found at the site. Their possible relationships, positioning and use have been determined based on comparative material, such as Assyrian reliefs of the period and fragmentary ivory plaques found at Hasanlu. Both show scenes of horses being ridden and driven. The arrangement of the bridle ornaments, bit and cheekpieces shown here was determined according to how they were found and recorded in the ground. The horse trappings from Hasanlu are important because they constitute one of the largest excavated groups of such material belonging to this period.

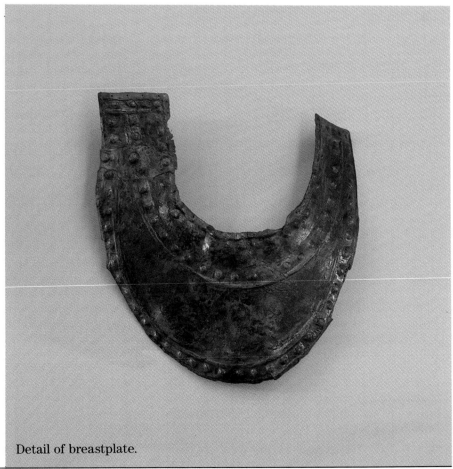

Detail of breastplate.

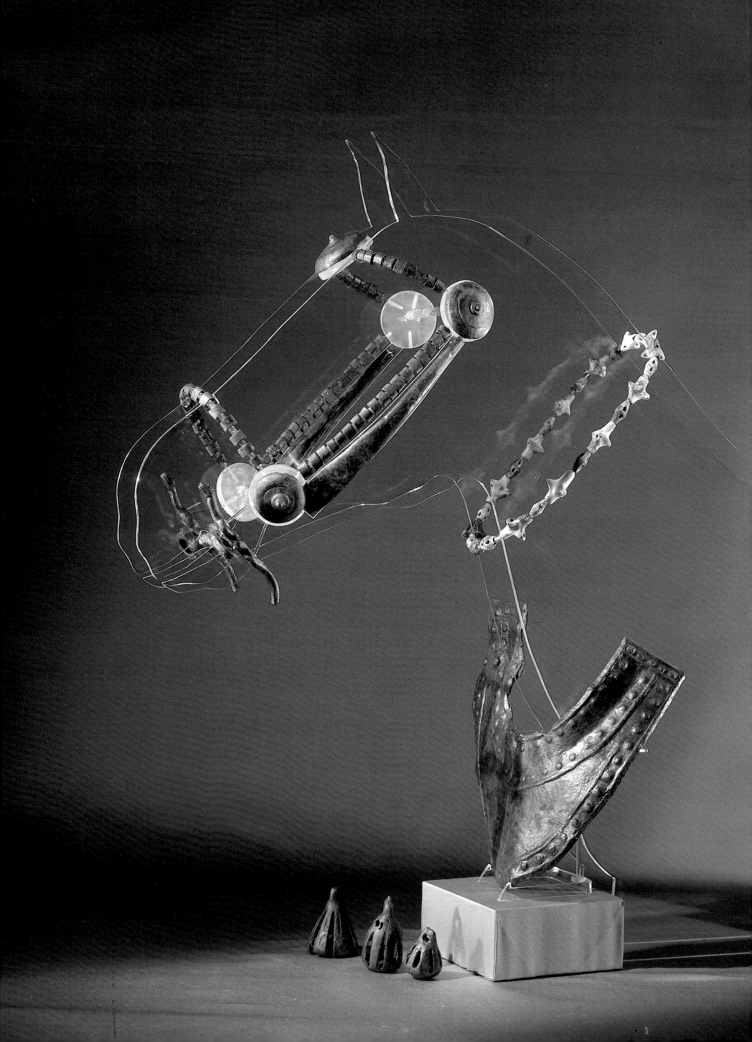

Drawing of an Assyrian relief showing a horse wearing a decorated bridle, a bit, cheekpieces, a necklace probably of beads, and a breastplate decorated with tassels and pendants. It is upon reliefs such as this one, from the reign of Assurnasirpal II (883–859 B.C.), that the arrangement and often the function of the Hasanlu objects must be based.

(From *The Monuments of Nineveh, from Drawings Made on the Spot* by A. H. Layard, Vol. 1, Pl. 32. London: 1849.)

were seated on the croup, the safest riding position on asses and onagers who have weak withers and carry their heads low. Such a position on a horse, however, delivers a notably rough ride, and is objectionable to the animal because of the pounding its kidneys receive. Given the primitive stage of riding, it is clear that, like the chariot, horse-mounted riders did not yet play a significant role in military operations. Kings sometimes rode horses, but the most common mode of kingly transport was a light, horse-drawn vehicle.

During the next period (1600–1000 B.C.), important technological advances occurred that led to the development of light, swift battle chariots. Foremost among these innovations was the rigid metal bit, which along with reins and improved harnessing afforded greater control of the horse. Chariots were now built to carry two or three people—a driver plus an archer or two spearmen—and became major battle vehicles. They provided a high degree of mobility and were ideal for fast flanking and pursuit on level open ground; they were essentially mobile firing platforms. Horse-mounted riders still played no role in combat at this time. The animals continued to be ridden from the "donkey seat," and the only significant improvement was the addition of a saddle blanket.

From 1000–600 B.C., horses continued to grow in importance. Skeletal remains indicate the presence of horses as tall as 60 inches at the withers and ponies as small as 40 inches. The best evidence for developments in this period comes from Assyria. Mules and oxen were used for draft, and crude pack saddles were employed for carrying captive women and children on mules. Men rode horses into battle for the first time in the 9th century B.C., still usually seated on the croup but occasionally in the horse seat (i.e., behind the withers), and using a saddle cloth secured by a girth. Both carrying warriors and pulling chariots, horses now reigned supreme in military combat. Kings also rode horses, seated on elaborately fringed saddle cloths and led by attendants. In the second half of the 8th century, the horse seat finally came into common use.

When horses were ridden in 9th century battles, they were bridled like chariot horses and operated in pairs. A warrior and his squire rode side by side. The squire carried both sets of reins and controlled both horses, leaving the warrior free to use his bow. Horses were far from realizing their maximum potential in battle, however, and the light two-man chariot was still very important. By the late 8th century B.C., riders sometimes functioned independently, sometimes in pairs. By the 7th century, warriors sat securely on their saddle fleeces or pelts, controlled their horses with a new reining system that allowed them to use weapons with both hands, and brought their mounts under check with improved bits. Mounted troops operated singly, and the superiority of horses over chariots for flanking and pursuit over all terrain was exploited. In consequence of the increasingly effective use of horse and rider, the chariot increased in size, height and weight (commonly accommodating a crew of four), but decreased in mobility and speed. These ponderous vehicles were pulled by four horses and served in part as stationary archery platforms.

Horses at Hasanlu

University Museum excavators at Hasanlu Tepe in the Solduz Valley in Iran have uncovered horse skeletons and trappings from a level dating to ca. 1000–800 B.C. Unfortunately, none of the trappings were found in position on the horses; however, comparison of

Although none of the horse trappings discovered at Hasanlu were found in place on horse skeletons, this drawing shows one possible arrangement of some of those objects. The use and position of the breastplate and beads are based on those shown for similar objects on Assyrian reliefs of the 9th century B.C. The arrangement of the bridle, bit and cheekpiece is derived from the position of the pieces as they were uncovered during excavation.
Drawing by Michael Garrity.

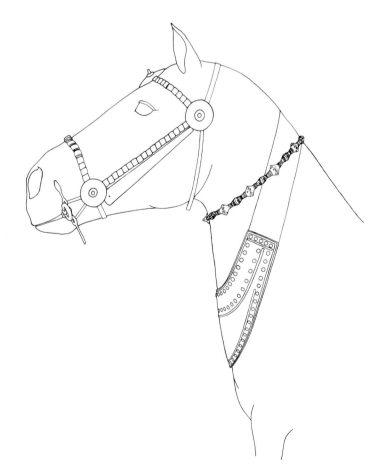

off on the warpath

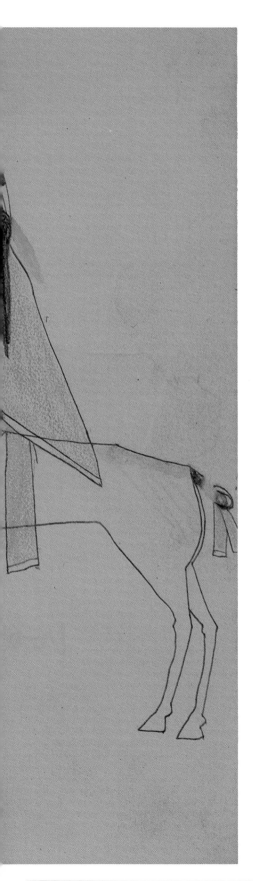

Pictographic ledger
Drawn by Matches, a Cheyenne
Indian imprisoned at Fort Marion
St. Augustine, Florida
1875
8016
21.5×17.6 cm.

The pictographic style of Plains Indian art goes back to prehistoric times. The drawing and incising on rocks, muslin and tipi covers was traditionally done by men to record historical facts and personal exploits. In the late 19th century, Plains Indians acquired account books and ledgers which they filled with realistic scenes from everyday life. Horses are frequently featured, along with warriors, U.S. soldiers and dogs.

Two hundred years after horses had been reintroduced into the New World by the Spaniards during the 16th century, they spread northward to the high plains of North America. The Cheyenne, having been gradually pushed westward by eastern tribes, also moved into the northeastern plains during the 18th century. The introduction of horses rapidly changed the lifestyle of Plains Indians, allowing them complete freedom of movement. They became horse nomads, following the seasonal migrations of bison.

the artifacts with contemporary Assyrian reliefs suggests that horses were both ridden and driven. Large discs, both in iron and bronze, were found in conjunction with horse trappings; these are shown in Assyrian scenes only on the shoulders of horses being driven. A burned wooden object which may have been a chariot was found along with the remains of a chariot pole and what looks like a spoked wheel with a few spoke ends still in place. Near this assemblage were objects that, by comparison to similar objects on Egyptian reliefs and in a scene on a gold bowl from Hasanlu, appear to be yoke saddle pommels. Furthermore, the gates at Hasanlu were of sufficient width to allow the passage of carts or chariots.

The bits which were found were all snaffles (two bars jointed at the center) and had separate cheekpieces which were usually tied onto the bit, although one class of bit pierced the cheekpiece. There is also a unique example of a bit cast in one with its cheekpieces. This became a common practice later. Copper or bronze bits were accompanied by cheekpieces of the same metal, while cheekpieces of horn were usually found with iron bits. Headstalls (the section of a bridle which goes over a horse's head) varied from quite elaborate to simple or perhaps completely undecorated. Some apparently had buttons at the junctures of the straps and in the center of the forehead. These buttons were sometimes accompanied by some sort of decoration on the straps and occasionally by an additional decorative rigid cheekstrap cover. A further but rare decoration on the face of the horse was a forehead plaque attached to some sort of backing, now lost. A group of glazed frit beads and copper/bronze discs for suspension were found with one headstall and bit group. These may have been used to decorate the chest of the horse. Beads of similar type were found elsewhere at the site in association with horse trappings and were probably used around the horses' necks, in the manner shown on Assyrian reliefs.

The largest group of bells, decorative hanging plaques, tubes and buttons, all made of copper/bronze, were found in association with a single, very elaborately decorated breastplate. Although it is not possible to know the exact arrangement of all these pieces, the large number of them would seem to indicate that they were used to decorate the horse's body. Some sort of ceremonial use also seems to be implied: the decoration of the breastplate itself shows that it was very special.

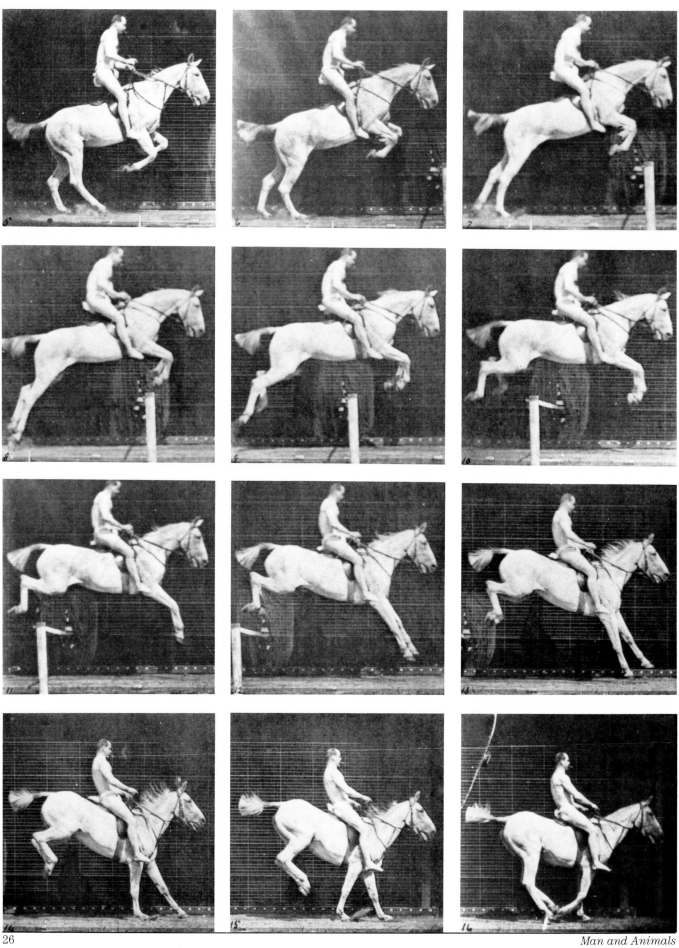

26

Further Developments in Horsemanship

The Assyrian empire collapsed near the end of the 7th century B.C., and was succeeded as a great power by the Achaemenid Persian empire, established by Cyrus the Great in 549 B.C. The Persians were great horsemen, but they appear to have contributed little to the advancement of the technology of horsemanship (equitation). Neither they nor the Greeks that followed developed a riding saddle. Royalty rode a heavy, ram-headed breed of horse, while mounted soldiers rode a smaller, lighter horse. As horses became more important in battle than ever before, use of the chariot declined further. A late, inferior form was the Persian scythed chariot, which had wheels equipped with sharp blades. Against undisciplined, unprepared troops, these chariots created chaos and panic. Against the disciplined Greek troops of Alexander, they were ineffective. Ranks of Greek soldiers parted to let hundreds of scythed chariots pass through; almost entirely lacking in maneuverability, these heavy vehicles were terribly vulnerable from the rear and were readily destroyed.

To Alexander belongs the credit of organizing the first cavalry, that is, mounted troops able to function as a unit with precision. Alexander's cavalry were capable of hand-to-hand combat, the Persian horsemen were not. At the battle of Gaugamela (331 B.C.), the Persian horsemen and infantry under Darius III greatly outnumbered those of Alexander, but they were routed by the superior Greek cavalry.

One of the greatest Greek contributions to equitation was the "Treatise on Horsemanship" by Xenophon (430–354 B.C.), adviser to Philip of Macedon. Even today, this book is a veritable mine of sound advice on horses and riding. It also includes the fundamentals of modern dressage, a system of progressive training to achieve balance, suppleness and obedience in the horse.

Saddle cloths were gradually supplemented with cushions or rolls, which made riding more comfortable but did nothing to improve the stability of the rider. Evidence for the first saddles with rigid frames, pommels and cantles (the hind bow) appears in China during the Han dynasty (206 B.C.–A.D. 220) and in Roman Gaul in the 1st century A.D. Surprisingly, the stirrup did not appear in the west until 477 A.D., possibly introduced from China, and was not in common use in western Europe until the 8th century A.D. The saddle and stirrup finally conferred the mechanical stability required for a rider to use a wide variety of weapons with both strength and accuracy. Thus it took, all told, nearly four thousand years for humans to learn to use horses to maximum benefit.

Recent History

Spreading north and west from the Near East, domestic horses were eventually introduced into every country on the European continent, along with England, Ireland and other islands. Some places had native stock, while elsewhere they had to be imported. As a result of importing, exporting and cross-breeding, it was not long before there were many different breeds of horses throughout Europe. Columbus brought the New World (Haiti) its first domesticated horses in 1494. By the early 1500s, hundreds of horses were being transported to the Americas from Spain, mainly by the conquistadors.

The first Dean (1884–89) of the School of Veterinary Medicine, Rush Shippen Huidekoper. The Dean was both a medical surgeon and a veterinarian.

(opposite)
Dean Huidekoper was photographed riding his own mare Pandora by Eadweard Muybridge, for the photographer's study of animal locomotion. The Dean was said to be a daring horseman.

(Courtesy of the University of Pennsylvania Archives)

Today there are over 100 breeds of domestic horses spread through many parts of the world. They can be divided into three main categories: light horses, heavy horses and ponies. The light horse, of Oriental origin, is a graceful running animal, bred for speed, and includes such breeds as Arabian, Thoroughbred and Standardbred. The heavy horse (Clydesdale and Belgian, for instance) is bred specifically as a draft animal—it can exert tremendous strength while moving at a slow pace. Its ancestors were probably the large, heavy horses developed in the Low Countries during the Middle Ages for carrying armor-clad knights (who might weigh up to 450 pounds). Small horses under 56 inches are called ponies; some well-known breeds are the Shetland and Welsh.

The modern sport of organized horse racing started in the British Isles, with earliest known account of such a race recorded in A.D. 1174, in the reign of Henry II. (A form of horse racing did take place in Greece much earlier; records show that mounted horses were raced during the 33rd Olympiad in 644 B.C.) In the early 1600s, horse racing was legally established in England, and in the 1790s, the English started the first association for registering horses. The first international horse show was held in Dublin in 1864, and in 1883 the first national show in the United States took place in New York.

The horse is without peer among domesticated animals. It can withstand extreme climates and exists today in all parts of the habitable world. It is also supremely adaptable and, unlike other animals, can be used by man for draft, sport, herding and transportation.

Bronze bit
Luristan, Iran
8th–7th century B.C.
30–38–11
L. 21.1 cm.   W. 1.0 cm.
Bits of this type were found in graves in some of the cemeteries of Luristan in the central Zagros region of Iran. They usually have cheekpieces, in the form of real or imaginary animals, that sometimes have short prongs on the inside to help control the action of the horse. This type of bit is typical of this region, while snaffle or linked bits occur further north.

DOG

Golden Retriever

This bitch is depicted in a scene on a wall painting from the tomb of Nebamun in Thebes, Egypt, which dates to the reign of Hatshepsut (ca. 1490–1468 B.C.). The dog is envisaged as having entered the afterlife with Nebamun and his wife. The type of dog is similar to the saluki, with pendant ears and a long tail; such dogs were used for protection, hunting and (as in this case) pets. Dogs, unlike all other animals including cats, were frequently given individual names.

This particular dog wears a decorated collar, probably made of leather of different colors.

(From *Ancient Egyptian Paintings* by N. M. Davies and A. H. Gardiner, Vol. 1, Pl. 15. University of Chicago Press: 1936.) Courtesy of the Oriental Institute, University of Chicago.

Ancestors of the Dog

The origin of the dog has been the subject of some controversy. The wolf, coyote and jackal have each been proposed as the wild progenitor of the dog. Each has dog-like characteristics, the same chromosome number as the dog, and each produces fertile hybrids when mated with dogs.

Although jackals (*Canis aureus*) and coyotes (*Canis latrans*) bear some resemblance to dogs (*Canis familiaris*), only wolves (*Canis lupus*) have had a geographic distribution consistent with known sites of early domestication, and only wolves have a behavioral repertoire resembling that of modern dogs. Like man and dog, the wolf has a highly developed social system based on a hierarchy of dominance within the group. It was probably this characteristic that allowed man to tame and domesticate young wolves. It thus appears likely that the wolf is the main, if not the sole ancestor of the dog.

More than 30 subspecies of the wolf, varying in size, skull measurements, hair color and other physical attributes, as well as in behavior, are recognized around the world. There is also considerable variability even within a single pack. A great many of the differences now seen between one breed of dog and another can thus be accounted for by the genetic variability present in their wild wolf ancestors. Man has simply selected for those genes which produce a desired type. In addition, man has preserved a number of mutations that have occurred in the 10,000 to 12,000 years since the domestication of the dog.

Domestication

Domestication of the dog probably took place in a number of locations and involved a number of different subspecies. The way in which the animal first entered into the human community is not known. It would probably have been a very willing camp follower, living in part on the leavings of Palaeolithic hunting groups. While

The domestic dog (*Canis familiaris*), like the wolf, coyote and jackal, has 39 pairs of chromosomes. The sex chromosomes are distinctive: in this preparation from a dividing cell of a male dog, the X chromosome is large and 'X'-shaped; the Y chromosome is very small.

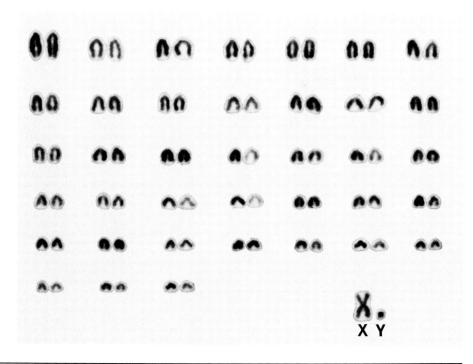

in the vicinity of these settlements wolves would also have been somewhat effective "guard" animals, whether domesticated or not. Disturbances from outside would have alarmed them thus alerting the camp inhabitants. We can reasonably speculate that Palaeolithic man found litters of wolf cubs, some of which were tamed as pets. These tamed animals were probably released to wander more-or-less free from human domination when they had matured and become difficult to control.

The genetic changes that are the hallmark of domestication came about gradually over a number of generations. By interfering with the breeding possibilities of the wild animal, man selected for reproduction those which were better suited to the intimate contact that domestication implies. The chief requirement for genetic change was the reproductive isolation of tamed wolves from the wild population. Although there undoubtedly continued to be occasional interbreeding with wild wolves, breeding within insulated groups of tamed wolves which were kept within human communities caused a drift in the frequencies of certain genes away from those characteristic of the wild population. Although much of this change must have occurred by chance, the first artificial selection may have been practiced by man at this early stage. Perhaps intuitively, humans chose to keep for their own those pups whose behavior was most easily controlled and those which had other desirable traits. It may have been recognized early on that certain pups had a special aptitude for tracking the wild animals used by man for food. By keeping and breeding these individuals, genes that confer a talent for the hunt were perpetuated.

Wooden figurehead
Key Marco, Florida
Ca. A.D. 1400
40700
Max. H. 32.5 cm. Max. W. at bottom 19.7 cm.

This wolf figurehead was wrapped in palmetto leaves, along with its separate ear and shoulder attachments, and buried in a swampy location in southwestern Florida. The shell mound site was probably inhabited by the Calusa Indians. Shortly before European contact it appears to have been suddenly abandoned, judging by the number of fine ceremonial objects that were left behind along with tools made of shell, barracuda jaws and shark teeth. The beautifully carved wooden pieces from the site are distinguished by their sophistication and bright colors. This figurehead was originally painted white, black and pink, but the paint has since disappeared.

Crest hat of wood, skin, cotton and teeth
Sitka, Alaska—Tlingit Indians
Late 19th century
NA 8507
Max. H. 16.7 cm. L. 39.0 cm. Max W. 16.5 cm.

This crest hat, carved of wood to represent a wolf, was made more realistic by the addition of real wolf scalp, ears and teeth. To the Tlingit, masks or headdresses like this one, when donned for a ceremony, endowed the wearer with the power or qualities of the creature represented. The wolf was known for its extraordinary courage.

The wolf was the hereditary crest figure of the kaguan-tan clan of the Tlingit, and only that clan could display wolf imagery. The animal probably figured in family legends—stories describing how an ancestor either dreamed or experienced an encounter with a particular animal or supernatural creature.

As generations passed, dogs of varying size and physical characteristics evolved in isolated groups associated with different human communities. When these communities moved, they took along their dogs, probably interbreeding them with other dogs and perhaps with wild wolves encountered along the way. At this stage, just prior to the dawn of agriculture and the domestication of animals for food, the dog was already clearly different from his wolf ancestors.

Diffusion

There is little doubt that the dog was one of the first domesticated animals. Bone specimens clearly distinguishable from those of wild canids and having features characteristic of present-day dogs have been found in the Middle East, Europe, Asia and North America at human dwelling sites dating to around 10,000 to 8000 B.C.

It has been pointed out by S. J. Olsen that the Chinese wolf (*Canis lupus chanco*) has a jaw bone with certain features closely resembling those of early North American dogs. These features are lacking in the North American wolf (*Canis lupus lycaon*) as well as other wild canids, suggesting that early dogs in this hemisphere were derived from the wolves of Asia and were brought with man in his migration across the Bering Strait.

Today there is a shallow sea separating Asia from America. These 90 kilometers (36 miles) can be crossed on foot during the winter and by small craft during the summer. But during the glacial period of the Pleistocene, roughly one million years, there was a land bridge here from time to time. This was many hundreds of miles wide and connected the Old World with the New.

During periods of glacial advance there were tremendous amounts of water locked up on the land. One consequence of this was that world sea levels were lowered, at times rather drastically, perhaps as much as 140 meters (420 feet) at the height of glacial activity. There is sound evidence that the Asian-American bridge, usually called Beringia, was open tundra at some time about 70,000 years ago, again between 50,000 and 40,000 years ago, and finally from about 25,000 to 14,000 years ago. It may have been during these times that Asian peoples came to the New World, forming the base on which later population expansion took place.

We can infer that the land bridge was not a totally inhospitable environment for humans and their animals. Many species adapted to temperate climates made use of it in their migrations between the two vast continents. These included deer, bison, horses and camels, as well as a host of smaller animals.

Beringia was warmed by ocean currents and would have been free of ice and snow during the summer. The shallow seas to the south would have created a rich environment for the foraging peoples living in northern Asia. We can imagine these men and women moving steadily east and south into a new continent. Many of them probably kept close to the coast because of the abundant food resources to be found there. (Unfortunately for archaeologists their camps are today underwater as a consequence of our relatively warm climate which has raised sea levels by the transferral of water from glaciers back into the sea.)

It was these Asian peoples who brought with them their only domesticated animal, the dog. Early dogs of America may have been descendants of these Asian animals. But, the wolves of America were probably also domesticated by these early immigrant populations, interbreeding and enriching the genetic base of the domesticated dog.

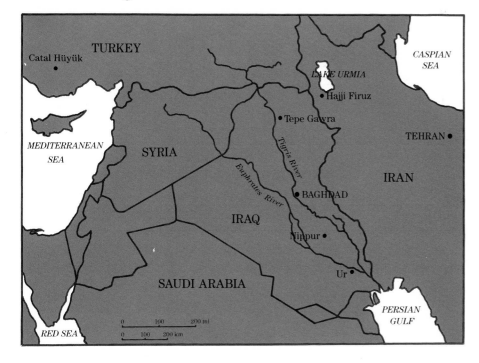

Archaeological sites in the Near East which have given us information on the history of the dog.

In Turkey today, large yellow dogs serve as watch dogs, protecting village houses and their occupants. Their massive heads contrast with relatively slim (and heavily furred) hound-like bodies. Prized for their fierceness and loud bark, these watch dogs are never treated as pets. This mother dog was photographed in 1982 in the village of Biraman on the Euphrates River.

Dog skeleton
Hajji Firuz, Iran
Ca. 1450–1150 B.C.

Hajji Firuz Tepe, located about 2 km. from the citadel at Hasanlu, was occupied during the Early Iron Age (Hasanlu period V, ca. 1450–1150 B.C.). The adjacent prehistoric mound was used as a cemetery. One excavated adult burial was accompanied by the three vessel types characteristic of Hasanlu period V: a finely made spouted vessel, an open bowl, and a very crude beaker. At the same level as the human skeleton, and perhaps associated with it, was this well-preserved skeleton of a dog. A second, less complete dog skeleton of the same physical type was found in a pit within the Iron Age settlement itself. The fact that these animals were carefully disposed of and were buried in close proximity to humans may be an indication of their value to people.

Stone stamp seal
Tepe Gawra, Iraq
Ca. 3200 B.C.
35-10-15
H. 0.85 cm. W. 1.6 cm. Th. 0.9 cm.

This stamp seal from Tepe Gawra in northern Mesopotamia is carved with the design of two salukis, dogs used for hunting from early times in the Near East. Seals such as this one, as well as cylinder seals, were used to secure jars and other objects whose contents were not to be disturbed. They were pressed into the wet clay that covered the opening of a container.

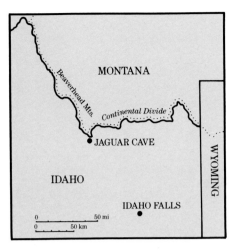

Map showing location of Jaguar Cave.

The Jaguar Cave Dogs and Other Dogs in the New World

Some of the earliest remains of domestic dog known in the world come from Jaguar Cave, a site situated at an altitude of about 7400 feet in the Beaverhead Mountains of east central Idaho. Occupation of the cave by humans seems to have occurred a number of times for short periods at the very end of the last Ice Age and at the very beginning of the postglacial period. The oldest hearth in the cave is dated to $11,580 \pm 250$ years ago, with a younger hearth dated to $10,370 \pm 350$ years ago (radiocarbon determinations made on charcoal). The cave was naturally sealed about 9000 years ago and, therefore, all remains found inside are older than that date.

In addition to a few tools, some 40,000 animal bones were recovered from the cave. Most (ca. 80%) came from the mountain sheep, but bones from a number of other animals, including coyote, wolf and dog, were also identified. Given the scarcity of artifacts from Jaguar Cave, the identification of dog bones came as a pleasant surprise since, together with the pit-hearths, they confirmed the use of the site by humans. On the basis of tooth and jaw size and shape, and the arrangement of the teeth, 11 of the 43 pieces from the cave were identified as dog, 28 as coyote and 4 as wolf. There were two sizes of dogs—one about the size of a modern-day beagle, the other about the size of a Labrador retriever.

The 4 specimens from Jaguar Cave identified as wolf stand apart from the other *Canis* jaw fragments because of their large heavy teeth and massive jaws. The possibility must be borne in mind, however, that the large "wolf" specimens may also represent wolf-dog hybrids. Recent studies of canid remains from archaeological sites in Wyoming strongly suggest that wolf-dog hybrids were present throughout most of the past 10,000 years, at least on the Great Plains.

Dogs, in comparison to coyotes, have large stocky teeth crowded together in a relatively short but heavy lower jaw. Unlike the coyote, the dog's upper jaw is fairly wide and has a markedly curved profile when viewed from below. The upper teeth are also short, broad and crowded in the jaw compared with those of the coyote, and they lack the sharply defined ridges characteristic of even worn coyote teeth.

Although other finds of dog remains in North America have been dated even earlier, those from Jaguar Cave constitute, for the moment, the single most securely documented source of evidence that at least two sizes of dogs were present in North America at the beginning of the postglacial period.

It is clear that Indian settlements from Alaska to the southwestern United States, Mexico and South America had dogs. According to one source, Indians of the western hemisphere had three types of dogs: a large wolf-like Eskimo dog, a smaller type of varying proportions and a much smaller animal of terrier size, usually with a shortened nose. Dog skulls with features resembling those of the Jaguar Cave dogs have been found in more recent sites, including the Basket Maker III-Pueblo I site near Albuquerque, New Mexico. These dogs ranged from a small, short-nosed animal with a wide palate and rather large brain case to a larger, longer-skulled form.

Other than the northern Eskimo dogs, there emerged from early dogs of the New World only one truly distinctive type that is recog-

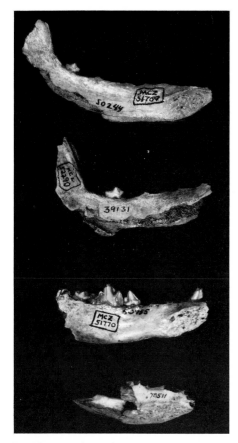

Dog jaw and teeth remains from
Jaguar Cave.

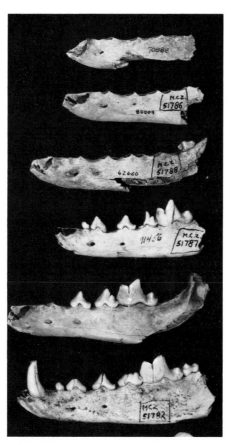

Coyote jaw and teeth remains from
Jaguar Cave.

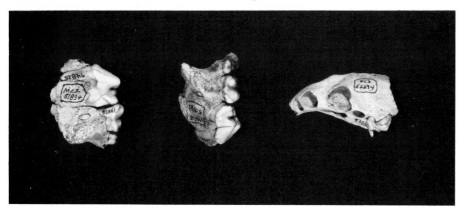

Wolf jaw and teeth remains from
Jaguar Cave.

nized today. In Mexico and Peru, the Aztecs and Incas, apparently
with mixed motives, developed the world's smallest dogs. Some of
these were undoubtedly the ancestors of today's Chihuahua. These
animals were used both for sacrificial rites and as a source of food.
According to one belief among early inhabitants of Mexico, the dead
cross a broad river to heaven on the back of a small red dog. Early
Chihuahua-like dogs were therefore killed and buried with the
dead. As was also true of the small Pekingese dogs developed in
China, the Aztecs made pottery figures and carvings of their
diminutive dogs and used them for mystical rites in the home and
temple.

herder looking for his ho[rse]

Pictographic ledger
Drawn by Matches, a Cheyenne
Indian imprisoned at Fort Marion
St. Augustine, Florida
1875
8016
21.5×17.6 cm.

Every Plains Indian family owned several dogs, which were cared for by the women. Dogs played an important role in the family, assisting with a variety of tasks. Their primary function was transporting supplies, either on their backs or with a travois, a carrier consisting of two trailing poles supporting a basket, to which a dog was harnessed. Dogs carried loads weighing up to 50 lbs. on their backs, or dragged a travois load of about 75 lbs., and could average about 5 miles per day with a heavy load.

Dogs also accompanied Indians on buffalo hunts. Trained to ignore raw meat, the dogs transported it from the butchering place to the village. Although it was customary among a few Plains tribes to eat dog meat, this practice was abhorred by most others.

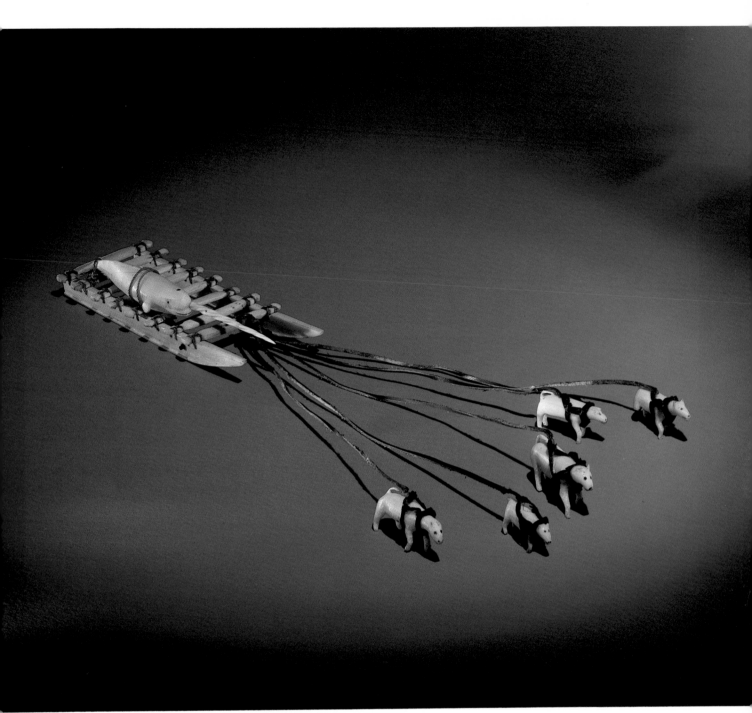

Sled and dog team model of walrus
ivory and twine
Greenland—Eskimo
Late 19th century
NA 9395
Sled. L. 16.3 cm. H. 1.9 cm. Max. W.
6.0 cm.
Largest Dog: L. 4.7 cm. H. 2.5 cm.

Eskimos are able to travel over long
distances of frozen terrain carrying
heavy loads with the use of dog-
drawn sleds. The average team consists of five dogs, with one lead
animal. The standard Arctic sled
dog is a hearty mixed breed that
has a weather-resistant coat which
can withstand the harsh climate.

In Greenland, dogs are also used to
sniff out seal birthing dens and
breathing holes, and occasionally
take part in bear hunts. In times of
emergency, they may be used as a
food supply.

The animal being transported on
the sled model is a narwahl, a small
whale prized for its unique spiraled
tusk.

Pottery red-figure jug
(oinochoe)
Apulia, South Italy
Late 4th century B.C.
L-29-67
H. 18.2 cm. Lip Diam. 11.6 cm.

Shown on one side of this vessel is a
representation of Paris, son of the
king of Troy, who grew up among
herdsmen and became a shepherd.
In this scene he is seated on a rock
outdoors, holding a shepherd's staff,
and accompanied by his attentive
sheep dog. Paris later ran off with
Helen, wife of Menelaos, thereby
starting the Trojan War which
resulted in the destruction of Troy.

Man and Animals

Dogs in Other Parts of the World

Dogs bred for different purposes were present in Europe possibly by 6000 B.C. By the time written history appears (ca. 3000 B.C.), an even greater variety of early breeds had been developed. Different breeds can be seen in representations in stone and pottery and in paintings from Egyptian, Assyrian and Greek sources.

The Origin of Modern Breeds

The modern breeds of dogs have originated in three principal ways. Some appear to have persisted from ancient times, more or less as they were produced by accidental or purposeful breeding of local varieties. The greyhound is an example. Members of the second group originated in modern times from locally-bred animals selected for particular characteristics. The Labrador retriever is one of these. The third group of dogs consists of those produced deliberately through the cross-breeding of pre-existing breeds, followed by selection for specific traits. Among the latter are some of the small terriers, the Airedale and the Doberman pinscher.

The greatest number of breeds have been developed within the past century and a half, since the advent of dog shows, official breed organizations and pedigree registries. The first dog show was held in England on June 28–29, 1859, at Newcastle on Tyne, in the reign of Queen Victoria. The American Kennel Club, established in 1884, now registers over 100 different breeds. Breeds range in size from the Great Dane and Irish wolfhound, the latter weighing up to 200 pounds, to the Chihuahua which weighs less than 5 pounds. The desire for novel types has resulted in the propagation of mutations producing lop ears, curly tails, short legs and short noses, as well as a number of variations in coat color, length and texture.

Marked variation between breeds is found in the shape of the skull. The skull of the saluki is long and narrow with no perceptible 'stop' (the rise in the skull at the base of the nose, producing a forehead). In the English bulldog, Boston terrier and Pekingese the skull is shortened, with a broad short nose and prominent stop.

A number of breeds have distinct variations in the length and shape of the limb bones. The dachshund and basset hound, for example, have shortened, bowed legs resembling those of certain human dwarfs. Their skulls, however, are not of the dwarf type, but more nearly resemble those of wolf-like dogs.

In addition to the remarkable variations of physical characteristics found among today's purebred dogs, there are also differences in behavior. The abilities to trail, point and retrieve game are well-known breed characteristics, brought about through generations of artificial selection. Anyone who has observed both terriers and hounds recognizes that these two groups of dogs tend to react differently to the same situation. The extensive genetic and behavioral studies of a number of breeds by Scott and Fuller indicate that, in terms of their behavior, dog breeds can be thought of as more or less specialized populations of wolves. Clear differences in reaction to fear, social interaction with humans and other dogs, trainability and problem-solving ability were found between breeds. It was also found, however, that the circumstances of early environment and training had a marked influence on these behavioral traits, and there was overlapping between breed groups.

Ceramic effigy vessel
Colima, Mexico
200 B.C.–A.D. 500
60-7-9
H. 13.0 cm. L. 26.0 cm.

The funerary art of western Mexico is characterized by zoomorphic effigy vessels. They were placed in the shaft tombs that are unique to this area as part of burial assemblages, and probably held liquid supplies for the dead. A small smooth-haired dog was indigenous to Central America, and effigies of it figure prominently in ceramics from the Colima region. The cultural significance of dogs in this period is uncertain, but they were probably used both for sacrificial rites enabling the dead to reach the afterworld, and for food.

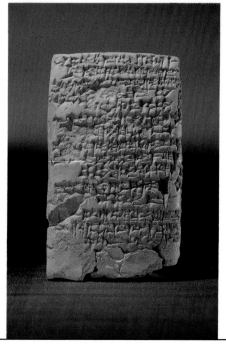

Clay tablet
Nippur, Iraq
Ca. 1800 B.C.
CBS 13106
Max. H. 9.8 cm. Max. W. 6.0 cm.

This tablet contains a dialogue between a supervisor and a scribe in a Sumerian school. In one part of the text the supervisor tells the scribe: "Like a puppy you have opened your eyes; you now behave as a person should." Frequent mention of dogs in literary and other types of inscriptions demonstrates that domesticated dogs played a major role in the everyday life of the ancient Sumerians and their successors. The earliest mention of dogs is on cuneiform tablets, found at Tell Fara in southern Mesopotamia, that date to 3000 B.C.

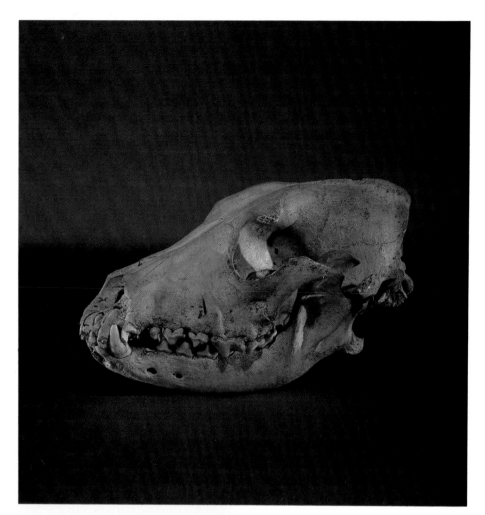

Dog skull
Tepe Gawra, Iraq
Ca. 3500 B.C.
38-13-71
H. 8.4 cm. L. 18.5 cm. Max. W. 9.0
cm.

This skull of a saluki was found in a
well at the site of Tepe Gawra in
northern Mesopotamia, in a level
dated to at least 3500 B.C. Salukis
are coursing dogs (which pursue
running game by sight not scent)
and were known to have been used
for hunting from early times in the
Near East.

Unbaked clay figurines
Ur, Iraq
Ca. 1600–1100 B.C.
31-43-488
H. 4.8 cm. L. at base 4.5 cm.
31-43-489
H. 5.9 cm. L. at base 3.8 cm.

Clay figurines of dogs, seated like
the ones shown here or standing,
were set beneath the floors of
houses. They were found singly or
in groups of up to five; some bore
traces of paint. Sometimes they
were placed next to prophylactic
(protective) figurines known as
"Papsukkal" figures. The latter
were placed in mudbrick boxes con-
taining ritual foodstuffs and were
set under the floors of houses near
walls or next to door jambs. The
presence of these figurines has been
taken to indicate the religious
nature of the structures in which
they were found.

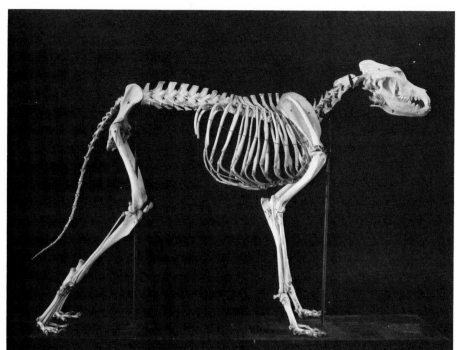

Great Dane

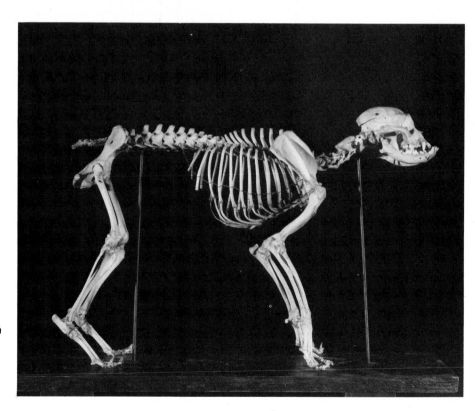

Boston Terrier

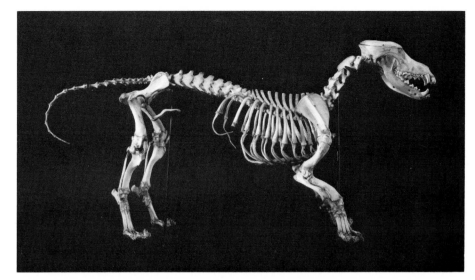

Bassett Hound

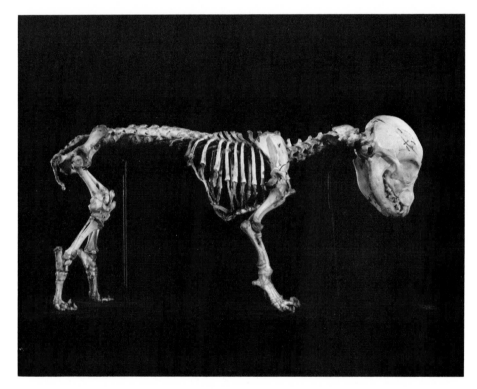

Chihuahua

The dog, perhaps better than any other animal, illustrates the profound changes that can be brought about by the process of domestication. Artificial selection for variations in size and shape has resulted in breeds of dogs that show remarkable differences in skeletal structure. Skull shapes vary from the long narrow wolf-like one of the Great Dane to that of the Boston terrier, which has a shortened nose and a domed cranium producing a prominent forehead or 'stop.' The basset hound shows the effect of selection for genes producing short curved legs. In the Chihuahua, there is an overall reduction in body size, while in the Great Dane overall size has been increased.

(Skeletal specimens are from the original collection of Dr. Charles R. Stockard)

Man and Dog

Thousands of years ago, man and dog hunted together as an effective team. Their relationship, based on mutual need and reinforced by similar social structures and patterns of behavior, resulted in a strong bond between the two which has endured. Man and dog probably interact with one another today in much the same way as they did at the end of the Ice Age.

Clay brick
Ur, Iraq
Ca. 2100 B.C.
A dog walked across this brick as it lay drying in the sun when it was being made. The brick is stamped with an inscription which tells that "Ur-Nammu, the king of Ur, has built his temple for Nanna, his Lord. He (Ur-Nammu) has (also) built the (city) wall of Ur for him."

Man and Animals

COW

Zebu

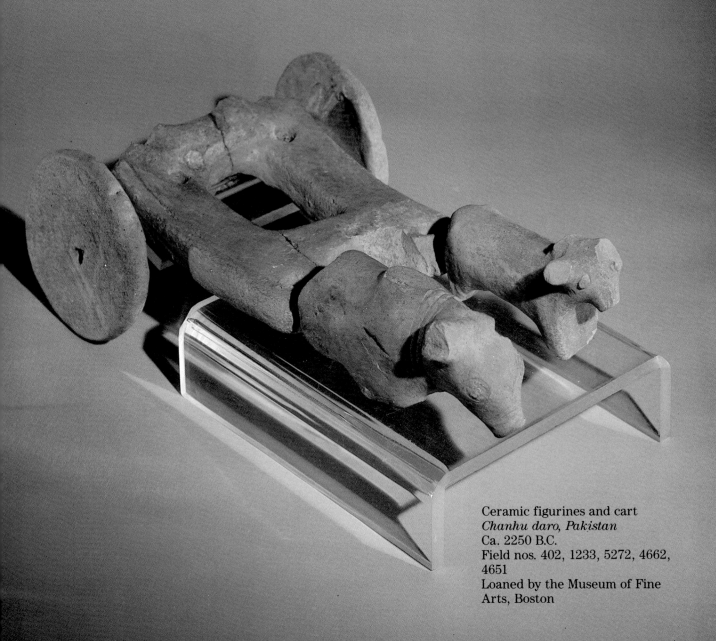

Ceramic figurines and cart
Chanhu daro, Pakistan
Ca. 2250 B.C.
Field nos. 402, 1233, 5272, 4662, 4651
Loaned by the Museum of Fine Arts, Boston

Early History of the Cow

The numerous modern breeds of domesticated cattle are derived from one or the other of two wild species: the extinct giant ox or aurochs, *Bos primigenius,* or the Asian animal, *Bos namadicus.* Ten to twelve thousand years ago, these large grazing and browsing ruminants inhabited the forests and open grasslands of the northern hemisphere, except North America. Although wild oxen were undoubtedly domesticated independently in a number of locations, the earliest evidence of domestication has been found at Çatal Hüyük in Turkey. This find, dated to ca. 6400 B.C., includes ox bones that are smaller than those characteristic of the aurochs, indicating that the people of this area had by this time brought about changes in the wild ox. In addition, shrines involving cattle horns found somewhat later in this region (ca. 6000 B.C.) indicate that the animals probably had religious significance for these people. Domesticated cattle from the Indus Valley in Pakistan date to the 6th millennium B.C. at the site of Mehrgarh. Ancient Indian traditions relating to cattle seem to begin here.

Early cattle were probably used first as a source of meat, hide

Steatite stamp seal
Mohenjo daro, Pakistan
Ca. 2500–1900 B.C.
Courtesy of James Blair, National Geographic Society

This stamp seal of the Harappan Civilization shows a male zebu along with script which has not yet been deciphered.

and bone, then for draft. In some parts of the world, they were developed for dairying. As in other domestic animals, selective breeding, particularly in western Europe and North America, has resulted in specialization: the Jersey and Guernsey breeds of cattle, developed in the Channel Islands of the same name, are used almost entirely as milk producers. Others, such as the Hereford and Angus, are bred entirely for meat. In contrast to the place of the cow as a food animal in western cultures, in many other parts of the world the cow is still used primarily as a draft animal, and perhaps to provide a little milk. Its manure is used for fuel and building material, and its flesh is eaten only when the animal becomes too old to breed and work.

The modern breeds of cattle have been developed from two principal domesticated forms: the European cow, *Bos taurus*, and the Indian humped cow or zebu, *Bos indicus*. Although considered to be separate species, the European cow and the zebu have the same chromosome number and can be interbred to produce fertile hybrids. In fact, the Santa Gertrudis, the Brangus and a number of other breeds used primarily as beef animals have been developed from crosses between the two groups.

Young zebus on a city street in Agra, near the Taj Mahal.

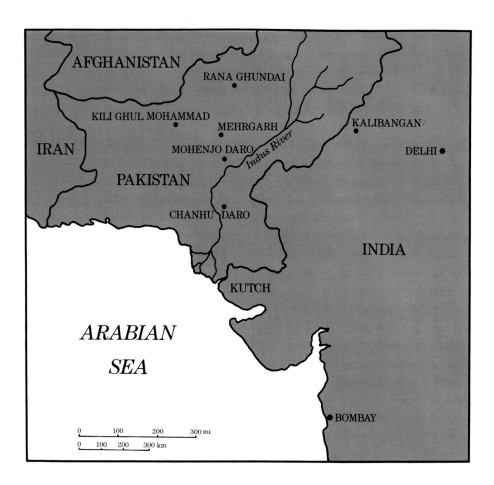

Map of India and Pakistan indicating archaeological sites where the remains of zebu have been found.

Cattle in the Indian Subcontinent

The domesticated cattle of India belong to the zebu group, which today consists of a number of different breeds including long and short horned types. All are characterized by a prominent hump above the shoulders and quantities of loose pendulous skin, especially under the throat and on the dewlap. This excessive skin provides a large surface area and is believed to act as an effective heat regulator, allowing zebus to better withstand a hot climate.

The zebu figures prominently in the archaeological record of the Indian subcontinent. Its remains have been found in the earliest village communities in Pakistan, Kili Ghul Mohammad and Mehrgarh, which can be dated to ca. 6000–4000 B.C. The abundance of cattle bones at these and other early sites tells us that they were of great value to ancient farmers in western India and Pakistan.

Early Cattle Iconography

Archaeologists and anthropologists have speculated that the cattle's central role in the ancient economy of the subcontinent led to its prominence in early iconography. Painted renderings of the zebu are the most frequent animal motifs on Copper and Bronze Age pottery from this region, and cattle figurines in terracotta, at times pulling miniature wheeled carts, are the most frequently encountered form of plastic art. Occasionally there are metal figurines of bulls, too, found at these sites. Much of this material seems to indicate the ancient Indian's appreciation and respect for the zebu's

Terracotta 'cake'
Kalibangan, India
Ca. 2500–1900 B.C.
Courtesy of the Archaeological
Survey of India

A deity with horns and a sprout of
grain on his head was incised on
one side of this 'cake' fragment.
This representation is similar to the
Great Yogi on the stamp seal from
Mohenjo daro.

Steatite stamp seal
Mohenjo daro, Pakistan
Ca. 2500–1900 B.C.
Courtesy of James Blair, National
Geographic Society

A Harappan stamp seal with
undeciphered script and a male
deity (the Great Yogi) seated on a
dias.

strength and productivity, a sentiment which is carried forward in
Hindu thought today. The ancient inhabitants of western India and
Pakistan took that sentiment into what appears to be a somewhat
deeper philosophical area as well.

From sites dating back to the formative period of the so-called
Harappan Civilization (ca. 2500–1900 B.C.), archaeologists have
recovered representations of a human or humanoid figure adorned
with zebu horns. This iconography is widespread during the Bronze
Age in the greater Indus Valley region of the subcontinent. In some
cases this horn apparatus seems to be a headdress. In other
instances it may well be that the ancient artist was portraying a
mythological entity, half man and half zebu. This iconography may
also indicate some form of worship of the zebu, possibly representing a "cow god." This, incidentally, is something missing from the
modern pantheon in India.

The most significant of these representations was discovered by
Sir John Marshall in the course of his excavations at Mohenjo daro,
near the Indus River in Pakistan. It is a square stamp seal made of
steatite or soapstone on which Harappan script (yet to be deciphered) appears. As can be seen in the illustration, the seal has
what appears to be a male deity of some kind seated on a low dias
or throne. His position is that of a yogi: the legs are bent double
beneath him, heels together, toes pointed down. His arms are fully
outstretched, with the hands, thumbs to the front, resting on the
knees. On the figure's head is an elaborate "crown" of zebu horns,
with a central element. He is surrounded by four animals above the
dias—elephant, tiger, water buffalo and rhinocerous—and two ante-
lopes below.

Cotton and silk embroidery
Kutch District, Gujarat State, India
20th century
84-6-1
Max. L. 1.495 m. W. at top 2.002 m.

The cow is often portrayed in contemporary Indian arts, as in this embroidery. Here the cow appears with one of India's many gods, Krishna, the eighth incarnation of Vishnu. Some of the many stories about Krishna concern his exploits in the forest as both a herder of cows and an enchanter of women. The notes of his flute have caused young women to desert their homes and herds of cows to join him in the pursuit of pleasure. Krishna's many seductions are seen from the Hindu perspective as a representation of the love of God for the human soul. The exploits of the Divine Cowherd have inspired many fine poets and pious souls.

Zebus outfitted for ox cart races in Mohenjo Daro, Pakistan. Photograph courtesy of George Dales.

Ceramic pot
Rana Ghundai, Baluchistan, Pakistan
Mid-3rd millennium B.C.
Loaned by the Oriental Institute (LI-907-1)
Max. H. 13.75 cm. Max. D. at top 21.25 cm.
Abundant remains of the zebu have been found in Pakistan's early village communities (6000–4000 B.C.). Not only were they important economically, but representations of cattle from the mid-3rd millennium B.C. on ceramic vessels and as figurines seem to indicate a special regard for this animal.

Marshall suggested that this ensemble could be taken as a Bronze Age prototype of the Hindu god Shiva. He noted that the headdress was reminiscent of Shiva's trident. Shiva, the *Mahayogi*, the great thinker, is often shown sitting in the manner portrayed on the Mohenjo daro seal, meditating and thus maintaining the universe. The seal also appears to have three faces, one frontal and two in profile. This is a common way for contemporary Indian artists to show the various aspects of Shiva. Of particular importance to Marshall's interpretation of this piece is that one of Shiva's manifestations is as *pashupati* or "Lord of the Beasts," protector of domesticated animals, especially the herds of cattle so vital to Indian life.

The presence of the four animals on this particular seal is not fully understood. Two are wild, the third, the water buffalo, was an Harappan domesticate, and the elephant may or may not have been controlled for community use by these people. Ivory is amply attested in the archaeological record, and the beast was certainly a part of the ancient Harappan landscape. It may be that the ancient artist was attempting to suggest that men and animals of all types were under the influence of this great yogi deity.

Granite sculpture
Chola Dynasty, South India
Ca. A.D. 1200
H. 49.53 cm. W. 78.74 cm.
D. 39.37 cm.
Lent anonymously

The bull zebu, *nandi*, is shown here as the vehicle for Shiva, one of the major Hindu gods, and his wife, Parvati.

Photograph courtesy of Eric Mitchell.

Man and Animals

The Economic and Cultural Importance of Cattle

Much of this is speculation, but one thing is clear. This and other pieces of iconography from the early cities of the Indus demonstrate that these ancient peoples were remarkably well adapted to their landscape, and thus there is much continuity between the ancient world and modern traditions. One enduring element seen over this remarkable span of time is the respect that man has shown for the cow. It is, after all, the most important domesticated animal on the Indian subcontinent. Cattle provide milk and meat, leather for a variety of products, and dung for fuel and fertilizer to the diverse religious communities of the region. Male offspring are the primary draft animals in Indian agriculture and play a critical role in the South Asian transportation economy. They are hitched to plows and may also be used to drive other types of machinery having industrial uses. Bullock carts are employed for transporting goods and as passenger vehicles.

Cows (adult females) have a special place in Hindu thought and sentiment that is quite apart from their economic usefulness. There are strong Hindu beliefs about the ritual and therapeutic powers of five products from the cow, the so-called *panchagayya*: milk, curd, clarified butter, urine and dung. There is as well a potent prohibition against the slaughter and eating of cows. It has already been noted that there is no Hindu "cow god"; still the cow is seen as the pinnacle of purity, nurturance and innocence, as something to protect. These feelings may be part of a broader philosophy, linking complex notions of femininity, motherhood, reproduction and continuity, out of which the cow came to acquire its position of importance to Hindus.

Copper figurine
Kalibangan, India
Ca. 2500–1900 B.C.
Courtesy of the Archaeological Survey of India

This copper bull was excavated at a Harappan site in northwestern India.

Over the past 15 years, the implications of the cow's special status for contemporary India have engendered a lively debate among economists, anthropologists, veterinarians and others. At issue is whether Hindu beliefs about the cow prevent India from effectively utilizing the animal as a major resource, thus adversely affecting the country's agricultural economy. Many of the participants in this debate, however, make assumptions about the usefulness of the cow which are fundamentally alien to the indigenous Hindu point of view and which ignore the wider ramifications of the animal's role. In early Hindu history, in more recent periods of Islamic and British rule, and in Indian nationalist politics both before and after independence, the cow has been a potent symbol of ethnic, communal, regional and national ideologies and movements.

Team of bullocks pulling a cart, near Lankhana, Pakistan. Photograph courtesy of George Dales.

Man and Animals

CAT

Tabby cat

Bronze figurine
Egypt, site unknown
1st millennium B.C.
E 2223
H. 8.0 cm.

This is the cat-goddess Bastet. She holds a sistrum, a musical instrument that is representative of her association with music, dance and relaxation. On her breast lies a pectoral bearing a cat head with a sun-disc above it. A basket hangs on her left arm.

The domestic cat (*Felis catus*) and the African wild cat (*Felis sylvestris libyca*) have apparently identical chromosome patterns. In both species there are 19 pairs of chromosomes. In this specially stained preparation from a young tomcat, each pair of chromosomes has a distinctive banding pattern. The X and Y (sex) chromosomes, seen at lower right, resemble those of the dog and other mammals. The other chromosomes are placed in 6 groups according to size and shape.

A domestic striped tabby cat, *Felis torquata*, whose coat and markings are similar to those of *F.s.libyca*.

Origin of the Domestic Cat

The cat family (*Felidae*) is widely dispersed in the world, its wild members being found on all the continents except Australia and Antarctica. The family includes the lion, tiger and cheetah, the lynx, bobcat and caracal, and a number of species of smaller cats found in Europe, Africa and Asia. A member of this latter group, the African wild cat (*Felis silvestris libyca*, also called the Egyptian or Kaffir cat), is probably the ancestor of today's domestic cat. Evidence for this conclusion comes in part from biological studies. The domestic cat (*Felis catus*) and *F.s.libyca* are similar in size and physical appearance. They can be interbred to produce fertile hybrids, and they have an identical chromosome structure and number, as determined by the most recent methods of study.

Domestication

It is not known when cats were first domesticated. A few cats have been found in 4th millennium B.C. Egyptian contexts, but it is uncertain whether they were domesticated. Some scholars believe that the existence of domesticated Egyptian cats cannot be demonstrated prior to about 2000 B.C., but further field work may change this picture.

How and why domestication took place is unknown. The cat may have found in human habitats a convenient source of shelter and food. Or man may have taken the initiative after seeing that cats were instinctive and efficient hunters of snakes and rodents, animals which have always plagued the rural villagers of North Africa and the Near East.

Diffusion of the Domesticated Cat

It appears that the domesticated cat spread outward from Egypt, probably over trade routes, to the rest of the world. An ivory statuette of a cat dating to about 1700 B.C. was found at the site of Lachish in Palestine. A late Minoan terracotta head, apparently of a cat, has been found on Crete dating to before 1100 B.C. Although cats were known on the Greek mainland from the Archaic period onward, they appear to have been rare curiosities. A marble couros base, dated to about 500 B.C., shows an animal that is in all probability a cat confronting a dog. The Romans were apparently responsible for the spread of the domesticated cat to central and northern Europe. Evidence for domestic cats has been found at villas and urban sites throughout Roman Britain and at the site of Vindonissa in Switzerland.

The cat did not spread to the New World until the 17th century, when they were exported to North America from England. During the same period they were also carried aboard British ships to Australia and New Zealand, areas which had no indigenous cats of any species.

The geographical spread of cats has been reconstructed to a degree through the modern-day study of genetically determined coat color types. The frequency of a particular color gene tends to be high in a localized area called a "focus," and to diminish gradually as one moves away from the focus. Lines connecting areas of similar frequency on a map are called "clines," and they define gradations of frequency of a coat color gene much as the clines seen on

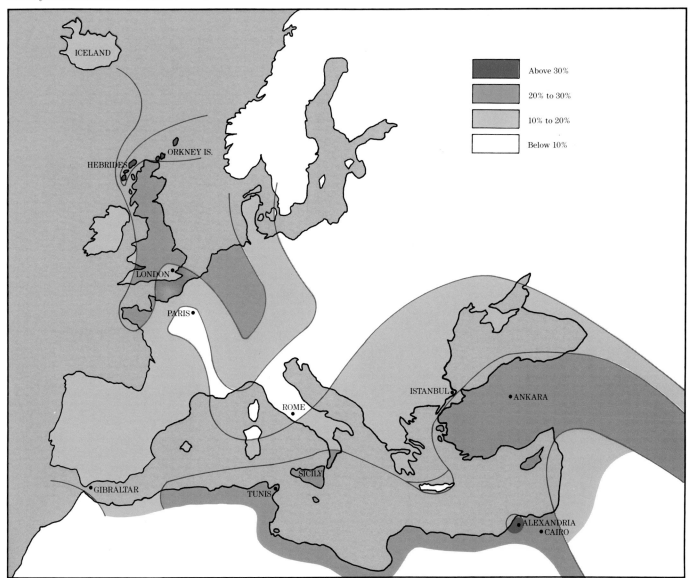

The African wild cat, *Felis silvestris libyca*, probably the ancestor of the domesticated cat.

Cline map showing the geographic distribution of the sex-linked orange gene.

(Based on a cline map by Dr. Neil B. Todd in *Scientific American* 231 (1977): 100–108.)

Above 30%

20% to 30%

10% to 20%

Below 10%

ICELAND

ORKNEY IS.

HEBRIDES

LONDON

PARIS

ISTANBUL

ANKARA

ROME

GIBRALTAR

SICILY

TUNIS

ALEXANDRIA
CAIRO

weather maps define gradations of barometric pressure or temperature.

Dr. Neil B. Todd has collected information on coat color gene frequencies in the cat throughout the world, and the resulting cline maps show a pattern that strongly suggests how the major spread of cats has occurred. The orange cat can be used as an example of this. The gene that produces the orange or "marmalade" coat color is located on the cat's X chromosome. This gene occurs in two alternate forms, called alleles. The more common allele, in most locations, produces a lack of orange color in the coat which is usually black; the less common allele produces orange. Since females have two X chromosomes, they can have three different coat color types. If both X chromosomes carry the non-orange allele, the cat will lack

Calico
Tortoiseshell
Orange

This scene is from a wall painting in Ipuy's tomb, Thebes, Egypt. It dates to the reign of Ramesses II (ca. 1289–1224 B.C.). Ipuy, a sculptor who worked on the royal tomb, sits next to his wife and receives funerary offerings from his son and daughter. The stains on the upper part of the garments are caused by scented fat running down from cones placed on the heads of the couple, a sign of good living and rejoicing. Next to the wife's chair is a pet cat, staring full-face at the viewer (an unusual pose in Egyptian art), and wearing a collar and a silver earring in its right ear as tokens of its mistress's affection. This adult cat is posed as stiffly as the human beings in this scene, but—as a welcome break from formality—a kitten sits in Ipuy's lap and toys with the linen sleeve of his garment.

(From *Two Ramesside Tombs at Thebes* by Norman de Garis Davies. Metropolitan Museum of Art, Robb de Peyster Tytus Memorial Series, Vol. 5, Pl. 25. New York City: 1927.)

any orange coloring. If one X carries the orange allele and the other the non-orange allele, the cat will be a patchwork of orange and black, the so-called tortoiseshell pattern (cats with white spotting as well have larger patches of black and orange and are referred to as calico). If the orange allele is carried on both X chromosomes, the cat will be orange. Since male cats normally have only one X chromosome and a Y chromosome, they can be orange or black but not both.

Dr. Todd's studies of the orange allele show that it has a focus along the coast of North Africa and Asia Minor, with the highest (36%) occurrence in Alexandria, Egypt. The relatively high frequency of the orange allele along the northern coast of Africa, in the Balearic Islands and along the Mediterranean coast of Spain sug-

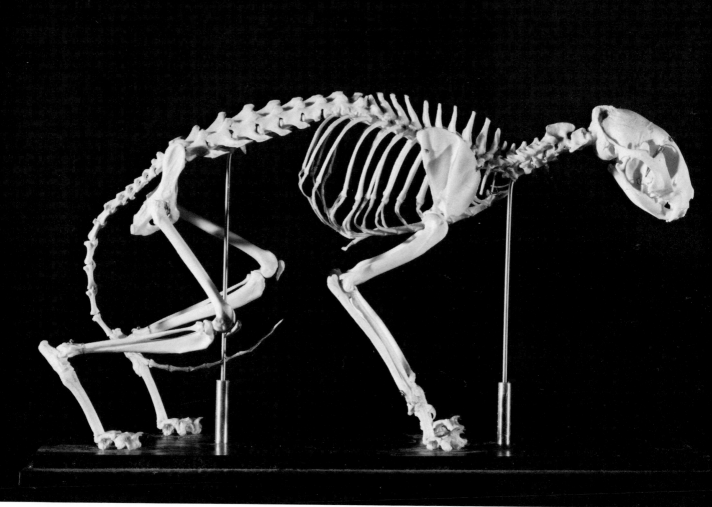

Except for some variations in skull shape as seen in the flattened face of the Persian or the elongated nose of the Siamese, the skeletons of all cats are similar. This specimen, from an adult male "mackeral tabby" domestic shorthair, is indistinguishable from those of cats belonging to a number of other breeds. The lack of skeletal variation in cats stands in contrast to the large variation in overall size and shape of the bones seen among different breeds of dogs.

gests that the gene spread from east to west over water, probably because cats were carried on shipboard. It is the habit of cats to take up residence on ships and to come and go at will, in some cases being left in port.

The Development of Modern Breeds of Cats

As with the dog, the breeding of cats in recent times has been marked by the development of a number of "pure" breeds that are recognizable by their coat color or other physical characteristics. In most cases, these have been produced initially by selection for particular mutant genes that confer a distinctive appearance. The Siamese cat, for example, has a recessive gene that limits the development of dark pigment to the hairs of the extremities. Other breeds distinguished by their coat color genes include the Burmese and Abyssinian. The Manx cat has a dominant gene that causes shortening of the tail. The Scottish Fold cat has a dominant gene that interferes with cartilage development in the ear, resulting in a shortened, folded-over ear pinna. The Rex cat has a double dose of one of a number of recessive genes that interfere with the cross-sectional shape and growth of hairs, so that members of this breed have a sparse, kinky haircoat.

Limestone door jamb
Memphis, Egypt
Reign of Merenptah (ca. 1224–1204 B.C.)
E 17527
H. 1.044 m. Max. W. 0.56 m.

This door jamb is from the palace of the pharaoh Merenptah. This unusual scene depicts Merenptah ritually slaying (with a combined mace and axe) foreign enemies, representing the actual victories promised him by the gods. At the king's side, his pet lioness leaps on the foreigners, grasping the elbow of one in her jaws. Whether such scenes actually took place is uncertain, but the lioness, a manifestation of Sakhmet the war-goddess, was an appropriate pet for the warrior-kings of ancient Egypt.

Although man has succeeded in preserving a number of mutant genes that confer a superficial change in the appearance of the cat, generations of selection have brought about much less change in overall size, form or behavior than has occurred in the dog.

Cats in Egyptian Life

Ancient Egyptians were familiar with many members of the cat family, some of which strongly influenced Egyptian culture and life. The lion and cat were particularly important.

Lions were hunted on the desert fringes of the Egyptian Nile valley until the early part of the 3rd millennium B.C. Human depredation combined with environmental change then drove them further south into what is now the Republic of the Sudan. In this same southern region, Egyptians encountered not only lions but leopards, lynxes and other felines. Both skins and live animals were highly valued and were obtained through hunting and as tribute and trade items from the indigenous peoples south of Egypt.

Lions were admired for their awesome size, strength and ferocity and were given a place in the royal court. They were not domesticated, but from late prehistoric times onward, they were caught and tamed to be companions to the king. Kept in special pens at the

This wall painting is from the tomb of Nebamun in Thebes, Egypt, and is dated to either the reign of Thutmosis IV (ca. 1412–1402 B.C.) or Amenhotep III (ca. 1402–1364 B.C.). This unusual scene highlights the complexity of Egyptian art. A nobleman hunts wild fowl in the marshes (a common pastime) accompanied by his wife and daughter, while a splendid cat perches improbably on bending papyrus stalks and seizes no less than three birds. Egyptian artists had a sense of humor, and the cat could be a satirical comment on the hunter himself, whose fine accoutrements and studied elegance suggest an equal improbability of success. The scene has a deeper level of mean-ing, however, for the hunter's regalia and other details indicate he is re-enacting the ancient royal ritual of fowling, representative of the sun-god overcoming the forces of chaos in the universe. In this context, the triumphant cat recalls the great cat of the sun-god, who destroys his master's enemies in the underworld as the god traverses it in his boat. All three themes—depiction of the 'good life,' subtle satire and religious symbolism—may be interwoven with each other.

(From *Ancient Egyptian Paintings* by N. M. Davies and A. H. Gardiner, Vol. 2, Pl. 66. University of Chicago Press: 1936.)

Courtesy of the Oriental Institute, University of Chicago.

Bronze figurine
Egypt, site unknown
Latter half of 1st millennium B.C.
43–12–15
H. (incl. tang) 12.4 cm.

This domestic cat wearing a beaded collar was probably a votive image dedicated to Bastet, the cat-goddess, for one of her temples or shrines. The figure is provided with a tang to set it into a wooden base.

Fragment of granite statue
Thebes, Egypt
Reign of Amenhotep III (ca. 1402–1364 B.C.)
E 2049
H. 76.84 cm.   W. 41.91 cm.

This is the upper part of a statue of the lioness-goddess Sakhmet. Although Sakhmet was the consort of Ptah, god of Memphis, she was also closely connected with the cult of the sun-god and in particular epitomized his punitive power. The sun-disc on her head refers to this connection. This statue was found with others at the funerary temple of Ramesses II (ca. 1289–1224 B.C.) at western Thebes, but had been brought there from the earlier funerary temple of Amenhotep III. Amenhotep III was particularly interested in coalescing the symbolism of the northern (Memphis) and southern (Thebes) royal capitals, and set up literally hundreds of statues of Sakhmet, goddess of Memphis, in the southern city, especially in the Mut temple.

Man and Animals

palace, lions were used for hunting and were sometimes depicted mauling the king's foreign enemies while the king simultaneously strikes these enemies with mace or axe.

The domestic cat's role in Egyptian life was primarily as a destroyer of pests, but it is also portrayed as a hunter, creeping through the marshes and up papyrus plants apparently to catch small birds for its master. Cat products such as fat, excrement and urine were among the more exotic materials used for medicinal purposes, probably for magical reasons and perhaps because they brought to bear upon the sufferer the curative powers of the cat-goddess Bastet (see below). The Egyptian word for the domestic cat can be approximately* vocalized as *miaw* and is a delightful example of onomatopoeia—the naming of a thing or action by a more or less exact reproduction of the sound associated with it.

Representations of cats as pets occur in Egytian art in the later 2nd millennium B.C., when they are shown sitting on their owner's lap or next to his or her chair, sometimes being eyed suspiciously by another pet, the fierce-tempered Egytian goose. Such representations also have another level of meaning, for the cat as pictured in funerary art was considered a creature hostile to evil beings; it could therefore be protective for its owner. The nature of the scenes of daily life shows that Egyptians admired and liked cats; so does the custom, attested quite early (end of the 3rd millennium B.C.), of sometimes naming women 'Cat.' A different but still affectionate attitude toward cats is evident in satirical drawings that, by a humorous reversal of roles, anticipate the basic situations of modern cartoons such as 'Tom and Jerry.' In these drawings clever and brave mice defeat or dominate cats; a mouse pharaoh in his chariot (parodying the great royal war scenes) leads a vigorous attack upon a fortress manned by cats, who clearly will be defeated; or an elegant lady mouse has her hair elaborately dressed by two obsequious cat servants. Elsewhere, in another satirical variation on a feline theme, a lion (sometimes given the name *rauw*) playing a lute raises his raucous voice in song.

Felines in Egyptian Religion

Both lions and cats were important in Egyptian religion, in ways that were interwoven with one another. There were several lioness-goddesses, such as Sakhmet and Bastet, who like the lioness herself were fierce fighters and protective mothers and who were appropriately cast in the role of mother of the sun-god. In Egyptian belief the sun was reborn daily. He had to be protected against chaotic forces that sought his destruction and needed to inherit from his mother an invincible fighting spirit so that he too could repel these evil beings.

On earth, the king was—at one level of Egyptian religious thinking—a manifestation of the sun-god, and the guardian and defender of the orderly universe the sun-god had created. The king, therefore, is sometimes shown as being suckled and embraced by lioness-goddesses and can himself take on the form of a great human-headed lion (the sphinx) who guards the temples and royal tombs and, by extension, defends universal order against the attack of chaos.

These concepts were accompanied by a related development, the identification of lioness-goddesses with the punitive powers of

*In Egyptian only the consonants are written down, not the vowels, so it is impossible to reconstruct the exact pronunciation of any Egyptian word.

Dark green faience figurine
Egypt, site unknown
1st millennium B.C.
E 3302
H. 4.8 cm.

This faience cat with black spotted body is accompanied by ten kittens—eight in front, one on her head, and a tiny one on her back! While this charming figurine looks like a light-spirited decorative element, it has a back loop and was meant to be worn as an amulet, presumably to attract the benevolent power of the cat-goddess Bastet to the owner.

Bronze figurine
Egypt, site unknown
First half of 1st millennium B.C.
E 3100
H. 14.35 cm.   W. 5.85 cm.

The cat sits on top of a stylized lotus which was the head of a scepter or part of a more elaborate object. It was probably dedicated to Bastet.

This fierce-looking cat sits next to its mistress's chair and turns towards a bowl of meat placed nearby. It is leashed to the chair leg, an unusual way of depicting a cat in Egyptian art. This and its exotic appearance suggest that it may be a wild cat, perhaps imported from the Sudan. May, the lady's husband, was "Harbor master of the Southern City (Thebes)" and therefore had excellent opportunities for acquiring exotic animals shipped up from the south. This is a wall painting from the tomb of May in Thebes, Egypt; it dates possibly from the reign of Thutmosis III (ca. 1490–1436 B.C.).

(From *Ancient Egyptian Paintings* by N. M. Davies and A. H. Gardiner. Vol. 1, Pl. 27. University of Chicago Press: 1936.)

Courtesy of the Oriental Institute, University of Chicago.

the sun-god. These powers were especially manifest in the uraeus—the cobra figure placed on the front of the gods' and kings' head-dresses—and with this the god punished his evil enemies and, on occasion, sinful mankind by means of disaster, fire and pestilence. Lioness-goddesses such as Sakhmet were identified with the uraeus and were particularly associated with the severe epidemics of sickness that periodically afflicted Egypt.

Yet, just as the small wild cat had been domesticated, so was the lioness-goddess in some of her forms. For in Egyptian thought the same generic deity could embody punitive and aggressive (against evil) power and also benevolent, nurturing power which benefited those conforming to the orderly universe. As a result, Sakhmet remained to the end of her history a fearsome deity, but Bastet—originally also a lioness-goddess—became transformed over time into the domestic cat. While Sakhmet remained the 'powerful one,' bringer of sickness, Bastet became the 'friendly' goddess, who cured sickness and sanctioned some relaxation of the normal restrictions of life—her festival was probably a 'feast of drunkenness,' like that of a similar goddess, Hathor.

By a reverse process, however, the domestic cat itself became, in cosmological thought, the gigantic and fearsome 'cat of the sun-god Ra.' Wielding a knife, it slew the monstrous and evil snake which threatened destruction to the sun-god and, along with him, the untold millions of virtuous dead.

The Cat as Sacred Animal

Bastet's importance increased in the 1st millennium B.C. because one of the royal dynasties (XXIInd, 945–715 B.C.) originated from her home city of Bubastis; thereafter, cat images appeared with increasing frequency in Egyptian art. Particularly common were statuettes of cats dedicated in temples of Bastet to be permanent reminders to the goddess of the prayer or appeal of an individual worshipper. Moreover, colonies of sacred cats were kept at Bastet's temples and, according to recent research, were perhaps ritually slaughtered, mummified and buried, in effect as dedications. Neither the cat nor any of the sacred animals of other deities were themselves worshipped. Like the cult-images of a deity, the sacred animals became objects of worship only when the deity—after the appropriate rituals and then only temporarily—entered the animal and dwelt within it.

Extensive cemeteries of mummified cats have been found. The methods of mummification were related to those used for humans. The body was placed in the desired position soon after death and treated with resin, or wrapped in bandages soaked in sodium salts, or perhaps treated in some other way. In some cases, the body cavities were filled with earth or sand. To produce a compact cylindrical mummy, the head was placed at right angles to the neck, which was fully extended, and the forelimbs were placed against the sides of the chest. The hind limbs were tucked up against the pelvis and the tail curled up between the feet.

Studies by Armitage and Clutton-Brock of a group of Egyptian cat mummies in the British Museum collection showed that the cats fell mainly into two age groups: 1 to 4 months and 9 to 12 months. These ages are unlikely to reflect natural mortality, and the authors suggest that the cats were deliberately killed at these ages, perhaps to cull excess males or to provide cats of the desired size for mum-

Bronze figurine
Egypt, site unknown
Latter part of 1st millennium B.C.
E 14284
H. 50.3 cm.

Many such figures like this seated cat have been recovered in Egypt, and most were probably dedicated at temples of Bastet in order to secure the favor of the goddess for the worshipper. This is a particularly large and handsome example, although the features have been somewhat coarsened by corrosion. About the cat's neck is engraved a bead necklace, from which is suspended a semi-circular pendant. The pendant is topped by a divine head, now obscure, but it may be a lioness head in profile with a sun-disc above. If so, the figure combines both the benevolent (Bastet) and punitive (Sakhmet) aspects of lioness-goddesses.

Cat

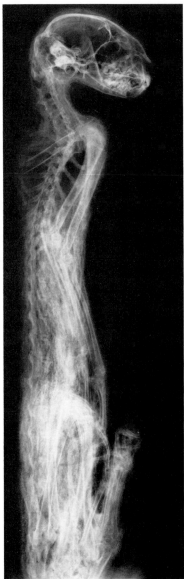
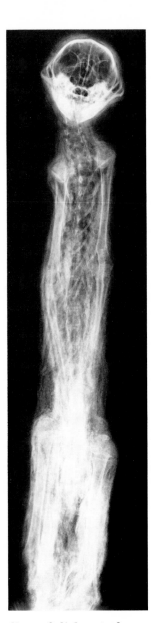

Cat mummy
Egypt, site unknown
Ca. 300 B.C.–A.D. 200
E 17636
L. 88.9 cm.

X-rays of this elaborately wrapped mummy reveal that it contains what is probably a cat (some cat "mummies" were actually empty shells), that it was perhaps immature, and that it may have suffered a skull fracture. Recent research indicates that immature cats were ritually killed and presented to Bastet, the cat goddess, as votive offerings.

mification. This surmise is supported by the finding of dislocated neck bones in a number of the animals. It is possible that the priests bred and reared cats in large numbers, killed them, perhaps by strangling, and made them into mummies to be sold to the populace as votive offerings. It is apparently these offerings that were excavated in vast numbers from their sacred repositories at Bubastis and Beni Hasan during the last century. Much of the contents of these cemeteries was sold for fertilizer. One consignment of 19 tons, shipped to England, is estimated to have contained nearly 80,000 mummified cats.

Egyptian attitudes about felines varied according to context. Lion deities were powerful and venerated, but Egyptians also hunted lions to death and could envisage them as representatives of chaotic, evil force as well as agents of divine retribution. As for domesticated cats, the mummified ones were in part sacrificial animals, the ritual slaughter of which was pleasing to Bastet; but the ordinary house cat was not intended for such sacrifice and, because of the link between Bastet and cats in general, the goddess was also pleased if they were protected from danger and ceremonially mourned after their death.

THE SCHOOL OF VETERINARY MEDICINE

The new building of the Veterinary
Hospital of the University of Penn-
sylvania (VHUP), completed in 1981.
Photograph by Bruce Stromberg.

Clinic: original building, ca. 1887. Dean Rush Shippen Huidekoper is in the white apron.

Founding of the Veterinary Department

Although a few distinguished physicians and educators had cited the desirability of having veterinary medicine taught at the University of Pennsylvania, it was not until a persistent farm manager appeared on the scene that some definitive action was taken. Mr. Horace Smith was the manager of a horse farm in what is now West Philadelphia, and he was very displeased with the level of veterinary service then available. He had good reason for concern because veterinary clinical medicine in the late 1800s was often in the hands of individuals with little or no formal education. The treatment of animal disease was crude and not infrequently barbarous.

Beginning in about 1877, Mr. Smith carried on a voluminous correspondence with members of the University of Pennsylvania faculty, various agricultural associations and members of the state government. His campaign focused on the very logical idea that the best way to improve veterinary service was to provide an educational system for aspiring veterinarians, preferably in association with a university.

In 1882, the medical faculty and the trustees of the University of Pennsylvania took note of Smith's entreaties and passed resolutions designed to create a Veterinary Department when money became available. In 1883 two benefactors contributed $20,000, and construction of a building was begun at 36th and Pine Streets, now the site of the Medical Laboratories Building. The structure was completed in 1884 at a cost of about $16,500, and it was equipped for approximately $350!

On October 2, 1884, twenty-nine matriculants joined thirteen faculty in opening what is now the second oldest veterinary school in the United States. Nine of the original faculty had M.D. degrees. It is entirely fitting that the Veterinary Department came about through the combined efforts of Mr. Smith, an individual interested in the care of animals, and the Medical School, since this set the basic mission of the School for the next century. The primary function of the Veterinary School has always been to provide, and improve, the health care of animals. It has met this responsibility by establishing an educational

system that gives the student a firm foundation in the basic principles of medical science, principles that are common to both human and animal medicine. The enduring relationship of the Schools of Medicine and Veterinary Medicine typifies the concept of "one medicine" at the University of Pennsylvania. In this respect the Veterinary School at Penn is different from nearly all other veterinary schools, most of which were established in association with agricultural schools.

An anatomy class of 1896, in the original building of the Veterinary School.
(Photograph courtesy of H. Ruth Frantz)

Early History

The opening of the Veterinary Department and its associated clinic resulted in an immediate improvement in the level of veterinary practice in Philadelphia and its environs. Horses, which provided power for transportation and farm work, were the most numerous animals seen in the clinic. There were, however, many farms surrounding the city, and before long cattle, sheep and pigs appeared. In 1890, the clinical service available at the new School was completed by the establishment of a Small Animal Section to care for dogs, cats and other companion animals.

Not only did the Veterinary Department provide the immediate area with better health care for animals, it also played a vital role on the national scene. At the time the School was created, and extending

Veterinarians in the garb used for work with foot and mouth disease in cattle, ca. 1909. Dean Leonard Pearson is third from right.

Students and clinical staff in courtyard of Veterinary School, ca. 1910.

into the 20th century, disease was devastating the livestock population of the young nation, and threatening the animal protein supply for the burgeoning cities. Early graduates from Penn joined veterinarians from other new veterinary schools in stemming the tide of this frightful loss, both in the field as practitioners and in important positions in government regulatory agencies.

During its first six decades the Veterinary School was known primarily for its educational program which produced a body of outstanding practitioners and individuals who made important contributions at other educational institutions and agencies. With a few exceptions little original research was done during this period; the faculty was not research oriented, and there was little money available for this purpose. Beginning in the 1950s, individuals having the necessary training and an interest in research began to assemble on the faculty. These individuals were able to attract the federal and private funds that became available for research after World War II.

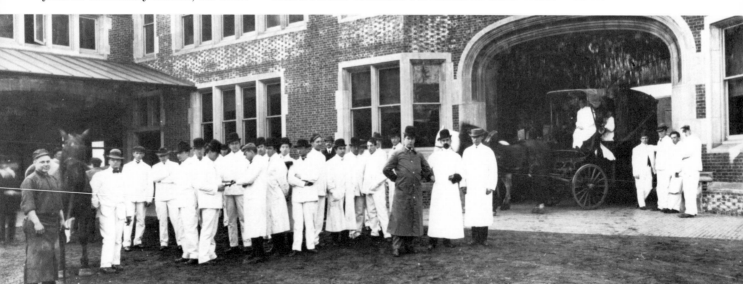

Man and Animals

The School in 1984

Today the School of Veterinary Medicine has an annual research budget which exceeds that of two-thirds of the medical schools in the United States! Many of the 125 or more research projects now conducted are directly concerned with providing new information about animal disease, but the School has also become the world leader in comparative medical research. This is research which contributes not only to improved animal health, but also enriches our knowledge about human health. Cooperative research involving veterinarians, physicians and other biomedical scientists is now a fact of life at the Veterinary School.

The School continues its tradition of leadership in veterinary medical education. In 1970 it introduced a revolutionary new core-elective curriculum. The core portion of this program presents basic information that is essential to all veterinarians, while the more than 100 elective courses enable students to selectively pattern their educational experience to their career goals. The Veterinary School also offers an extensive Continuing Education Program, enabling practitioners to keep abreast of new developments.

The School of Veterinary Medicine has two campuses. The urban campus is located in Philadelphia, on the main campus of the University of Pennsylvania, and it is primarily involved in teaching and research in the basic sciences and in providing health care for companion animals. The rural campus, New Bolton Center, comprises over 1000 acres in the rich agricultural area of Chester County, Pennsylvania, near Kennett Square. New Bolton Center is world renowned for its research and clinical work on horses and farm animals.

The School of Veterinary Medicine pioneered the development of clinical specialties, and its present role as the world leader in this field is reflected in the scope and sophistication of the clinical services offered by its two hospitals. The Veterinary Hospital of the University of Pennsylvania (VHUP), situated in Philadelphia, sets the world standard for health care for companion animals and wild and exotic animals. VHUP offers specialties in animal behavior, cardiology, dermatology, medical genetics, pediatrics, reproduction, respiratory diseases, neurology, oncology, orthopedics, radiology and soft tissue surgery. A 24-hour emergency service and special clinics for wild animals, exotic animals and dental medicine are offered in VHUP, along with the service of a social worker who is available for consultation with clients. VHUP has facilities for hospitalizing 250 animals.

New Bolton Center provides a complete array of medical and surgical services for farm animals and horses in the George D. Widener Hospital for Large Animals, and conducts an extensive research program on diseases of these animals. Special facilities at the New Bolton Center include the C. Mahlon Kline Center for Orthopedics and Rehabilitation, the Georgia and Philip Hofmann Research Center for Animal Reproduction, the Comparative Leukemia Research Unit, the Equine Outpatient Clinic and the Animal Health Economics Unit.

Cat with nurse attendant, VHUP, 1982.

Dr. Robert H. Whitlock examines horse teeth, New Bolton Center.

Diagnosis and care at the
Small Animal Hospital
(VHUP)

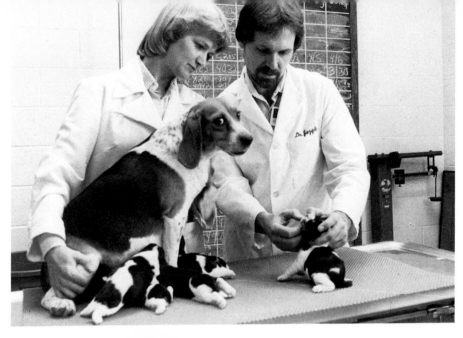

Veterinary pediatrician and obstetrician examining a mother and her new family.

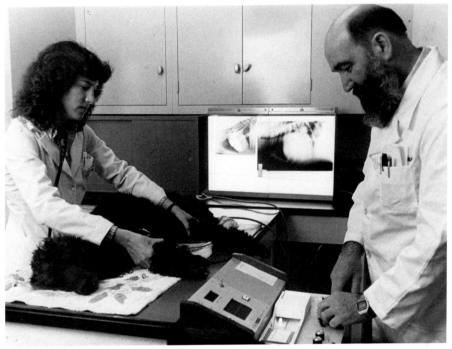

Veterinary cardiologist and student take an electrocardiogram on a standard poodle with heart disease.

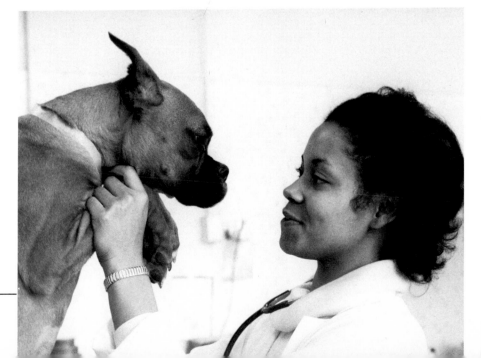

Veterinary student and patient see eye to eye.

Bovine surgery,
New Bolton Center.

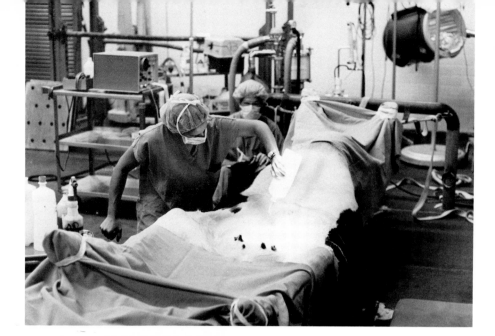

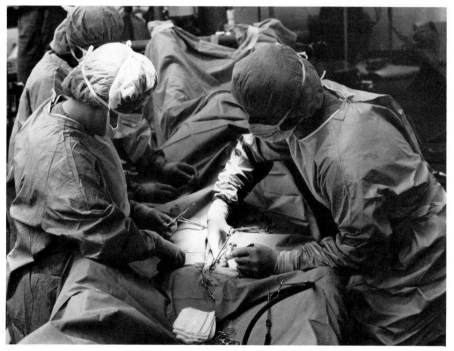

In 1984 the University of Pennsylvania's School of Veterinary
Medicine celebrates a century of achievement and its arrival at the
threshold of a bright and expanded future of significant contributions to animal and human health. In its first 100 years the School,
to a remarkable degree, has molded the study and practice of veterinary medicine in the nation and in the world. It has played a vital
role in the veterinary profession's contributions to the present
system of sophisticated health care for animals. Through its extensive imaginative research efforts the School continues to make
important contributions in such areas as improvement of breeds,
and increased productivity and performance in animals. The partici-
pation of the Veterinary School, with The University Museum of the
University of Pennsylvania, in presenting the exhibition *Man and
Animals: Living, Working and Changing Together* reflects the
School's broad commitment to furthering our knowledge of the
evolving picture of the interrelationship of man and animals.

BIBLIOGRAPHY

Horse

Littauer, M. A., and J. H. Crouwel
  1979 *Wheeled Vehicles and Ridden Animals in the Ancient Near East.* Leiden and Koln: E. J. Brill.

Piggott, Stuart
  1983 *The Earliest Wheeled Transport.* From the Atlantic Coast to the Caspian Sea. Ithaca: Cornell University Press.

Dog

Lawrence, B.
  1968 Antiquity of large dogs in North America. *Tebiwa* 11:43–45.

Olsen, Stanley J.
  1974 Early Domestic Dogs in North America and Their Origins. *Journal of Field Archaeology* 1:343–45.

Olsen, S. J., and J. W. Olsen
  1977 The Chinese Wolf, Ancestor of New World Dogs. *Science* 197:533–35.

Scott, J. P., and J. L. Fuller
  1965 *Genetics and the Social Behavior of the Dog.* Chicago and London: University of Chicago Press.

Sydney, H. C.
  1979 *Essentials of the Standards at a Glance.* (3d ed.) Providence, RI: Essential Publishers, Inc.

Cow

Sankalia, H. D.
  1974 *The Prehistory and Protohistory of India and Pakistan.* Poona, India: Deccan College Postgraduate and Research Institute.

Cat

Armitage, P. L., and J. Clutton-Brock
  1981 A radiological and histological investigation into the mummification of cats from ancient Egypt. *Journal of Archaeological Science* 8:185–96.

Todd, N. B.
  1977 Cats and Commerce. *Scientific American* 231:100–108.

Wurster-Hill, D. H., and W. R. Centerwall
  1982 The interrelationships of chromosome banding patterns in canids, mustelids, hyena, and felids. *Cytogenetics and Cell Genetics* 34:178–92.

General Reference

American Kennel Club
  1979 *The Complete Dog Book.* New York, NY: Howell Book House.

Beadle, M.
  1977 *The Cat: History, Biology and Behavior.* New York, NY: Simon and Schuster

Clutton-Brock, J.
  1981 *Domesticated Animals from Early Times.* Austin: University of Texas Press.

Fiennes, R., and A. Fiennes
  1968 *The Natural History of Dogs.* New York: Bonanza Books.

Matolcsi, J. (ed.)
  1973 *Domestikations forschung und Geschicte der Hanstiere.* Budapest: Akademiai Kiado.

Zeuner, F. E.
  1963 *A History of Domesticated Animals.* London: Hutchison.